Here's what others are saying about *Raising More Money*® . . .

This approach has caused nothing short of an organizational transformation for us. In the process, we have raised more money than we ever dreamed—a direct benefit to the elderly people we serve.

Norman Murphy, Ph.D.
Director of Community Development
Friends for Life
Waco, TX

Terry's approach took the fear out of fundraising. Her model gave us the system and the courage to launch a long-overdue major gifts campaign. Now our loyal supporters are thanking us!

Tom Luhnow, Executive Director
Seattle Men's Chorus
Seattle, WA

The *Raising More Money*® methodology has been an invaluable resource as we prepare to launch a major capital campaign and solidify our base of individual donors. Our entire board has been inspired by Terry's common-sense, proven model for fundraising.

Joanne Lin
Board Vice President of Development
Ronald McDonald House at Stanford
Palo Alto, CA

The guiding principles of *Raising More Money*® offered us a compassionate approach to funding the bold venture of landmine removal in Vietnam. We designed a system for citizens from around the world to participate in reversing this legacy of war which raised $230,000 USD in ten months.

Jerilyn Brusseau, Founding Director
PeaceTrees Vietnam
Bainbridge Island, WA

Our board loved this approach. It reconnected them to their passion for the organization and helped them play an essential role in the fund raising process without ever having to ask their friends for money. Even more importantly, our community has responded in the most positive ways. So many more people now think of themselves as members of our agency family.

Craig Bowman, Executive Director
Sexual Minority Youth Assistance
*   League (SMYAL)*
Washington, D.C.

Terry's model for fund raising, developed at a school, can be modified to work for any nonprofit. The principles she addresses are the very bedrock of fund raising.

Katie Ziglar
Chief of Development
Smithsonian American Art Museum
Washington, D.C.

RAISING
MORE
MONEY®

RAISING MORE MONEY®

A Step-by-Step Guide to Building Lifelong Donors

TERRY AXELROD

Boylston Books Ltd.
SEATTLE, WASHINGTON

ISBN 0-9700455-4-9

LCCN 00-131777

ACKNOWLEDGMENTS

There is no question that for the work of the Raising More Money programs and the material that follows, I am most indebted to the extraordinary community—or better said, "family"—at Zion Preparatory Academy in Seattle, Washington. The visionary leadership and raw courage of Doug and Elizabeth Wheeler, Pastor Eugene Drayton and Coreather ("Mother") Drayton in opening their pristine jewel of a school to the larger world was a complete gift in my life and the lives of every single person it has ever touched. Their willingness, along with that of the dedicated and passionate "Friends of Zion" fund-raising-only "board," to let me experiment with those crazy breakfast tours (now known as Points of Entry), not to mention renting out that huge hotel ballroom for our first super-risky Free One-Hour Breakfast Event, led to the creation of this model which has now been adapted successfully by hundreds of organizations nationally and internationally.

What I have done, as with most new thinking, did not take place in a vacuum. Over the last five years, as the Raising More Money programs have grown and developed, I have discovered many others saying the same thing, often more articulately, about their respective fields. When applied to the field of fund development, their work sheds new light. The books in which they lay out their ideas are all listed in the Bibliography.

In particular, I acknowledge the work of Stan Davis and Christopher Meyer, whose book *Blur: The Speed of Change in*

viii   RAISING MORE MONEY

The Connected Economy validates the pace and complexity we have come to take for granted and the unique way we will have to package our "products" to capture people's attention and hearts.

Seth Godin's *Permission Marketing* validates, from the Internet marketing perspective, what we are seeing in the nonprofit world today: That the days of interrupting people by strong-arming them for their money are over. All fund raising needs to be done based on incremental levels of earned "permission" with each potential donor. The ultimate level is what he calls "intravenous permission," by which time we have earned enough trust from the customer, or in this case the donor, that we may ask for and receive anything of them.

Rolf Jensen's *The Dream Society* validates the need for much greater use of the emotional hook to engage donors. Most nonprofits err on the side of being too clinical and dry. Applying his work to the nonprofit world, we see that our donors will increasingly be looking to us to "satisfy their desire to feel and display emotion," to engage in "emotional jogging."

For training me in their brilliant technology to be able to distinguish models which can then be tailored and applied in widely divergent settings, I am eternally grateful to Landmark Education Corporation. And further, to Helen Gilhooly, who trained me to deliver a message powerfully enough to cause people to take action, rather than just think about it.

Next, to all of the participants of the Raising More Money program, including those first 25 brave souls who were willing to pay $5,000 each, believing that I had something of value to impart. They paved the way for hundreds of others who have taken this model to heights I never dreamed of.

To Ann Overton, my "virtual" editor, for her steadfast hand in guiding me through the overwhelming process of turning the essence of a workshop into a cogent book. I could not have done this without her.

To my husband and business partner, Alan Axelrod, for not laughing at me that morning in the bathroom when I told him it was time to take all that I had learned at Zion and turn it into a "class," and for his genius in making this message broadly available. More than one "romantic getaway" vacation was lost to a wife wedded to a laptop keyboard. And finally, to our new-reality teenage children, Sara and David, whose generation, I pray, will grow up knowing only the joy of true contribution.

TABLE OF CONTENTS

I am an unabashed lover of the nonprofit world. I have been a founder of three nonprofit organizations and, like most of you, have been involved with countless others over the past 30 years.

It wasn't until 1992 that I realized how much the reality of giving and fund raising had shifted. I had been asked to help raise funds for Zion Preparatory Academy, an extraordinary inner-city private school in Seattle, Washington. Until that year, the school had operated strictly on monthly tuition of $190 a month. The teachers had been promised raises, requiring immediate private funds of $500,000 a year.

In the next two-and-a-half years, we raised $7.3 million. Donors who truly supported the mission of the school made pledges totaling nearly $1 million a year for five years to be used for unrestricted operating needs. In addition, we completed a $3.2 million capital campaign in that same time, from those same new donors. That is a lot of money for any organization to raise, let alone one brand new at fund raising.

This small, relatively unknown, wonderful school had become the beneficiary of what we now call a new paradigm. All of the statistics I had been reading about the vast amount of individual giving now seemed obvious. We had seen those statistics validated right there in our bottom line. In fact, the fund-raising terrain of the past that most of us had become so comfortable with had completely shifted. There was a whole "new reality."

While we had come to take this new reality for granted in our personal lives, it had yet to spill over into the nonprofit world. In the midst of such abundance and passion, our beloved organizations were still suffering.

Once I adjusted my vision to this new reality, it became clear to me that nonprofit organizations needed to be asking for money in a whole new, much more personalized, way. People were ready to hear the straight story. They wanted to know the facts. They wanted to become involved, but not in the tidy, already-set volunteer job descriptions we had in mind for them. These donors could bring us state-of-the-art programs and armies of volunteers. Many wanted to roll up their sleeves and get personally involved, as did their children and families.

They were perfectly comfortable giving money for unrestricted operating needs. They were happy to make large gifts to an endowment, even as their first gift. They paid their pledges off several years early and made bigger ones. They got their friends involved. Many asked how they could serve on our board. They were prepared to be loyal to us.

In short, they wanted to contribute, in the old-fashioned sense of the word. They didn't need all the bells and whistles—just the facts, the raw emotion, and a clear sense that their contribution would make a difference.

You could call them the new breed of individual donors. They are the donors who believe so strongly in what you are doing that they feel you are doing their work. That very same mission statement you have posted on your wall may be their mission as well. And, as such, they want to give in order to support it. I repeat: these donors *want* to give.

In the first session of our Raising More Money workshops, we ask people to imagine leaving their organization today and not coming back for 20 years. There you are, walking in the door, 20 years from now. No one recognizes you. As you walk around, you notice a distinct change has taken place. It is palpable: No one seems to be suffering about the money. Everyone is fully engaged in fulfilling on the vital mission of the organization. Programs and services have vastly expanded, people in need are receiving the services. The offices look great. There is an air of prosperity about the place that was never there back in your day.

As you talk with these new folks, it becomes crystal clear they no longer are worrying about the money. The once all-pervasive concern for financial survival is nowhere to be found.

You cannot restrain yourself from asking the obvious question: "What happened? No one here today seems particularly concerned about not having enough money?"

"Oh, that?" they say. "We handled that about 15 years ago."

Stunned, you blurt out, "Fifteen years ago? What happened then?"

What if the answer to that question was yours to fill in? What if you were the person who could cause the breakthrough needed to give your organization a self-sustaining fund-raising system, the person who could bring your organization into the new reality? What if your legacy was to have lifted their sights way beyond surviving—to thriving?

A major shift that forever alters the course of your funding is wanted and needed right now. This book is designed to give you the tools to bring your organization into the new reality of individual giving, of building a system of lifelong donors.

True to its name, a paradigm shift alters everything in its path. Futurist Joel Barker says, "When the paradigm shifts, everyone goes back to zero. Your past successes no longer count...they guarantee you nothing. In fact, your successful past can block your vision of the future."

In other words, the paradigm shift is the great equalizer. Every organization has been starting over. What they are all discovering, from the largest multi-billion dollar nonprofits down to the tiniest start-ups, is that individual giving is a shoe that fits for everyone. Every single nonprofit organization has individuals who do or could believe in its mission—individuals who would be ready to support that organization, if only someone would court them properly.

Fortunately, many more nonprofits are waking up to the new reality—mostly out of necessity. In the aftershocks of radical shifts in United Way and government funding of the last decade, most organizations have realized they need to reduce their dependence on large, single-source funders and diversify into the world of individual donors.

Likewise, many organizations that have been heavily dependent on direct mail or telemarketing are finally waking up to what their vendors have been telling them for years: these vehicles were designed to *acquire* new donors, not to grow them into lifelong major donors. At a certain point, someone within the organization has to actually talk to and get to know these donors to learn what motivates them to give to this organization, and what it would take to have them give more.

In the old reality, since fund raising from individuals was not a necessity, no one really had to know how to do it. Executive directors and founders of organizations had the luxury of being strictly mission-driven. Any 'knack' for fund raising was considered a bonus.

Most people still believe fund raising is an inherited genetic trait. Either you have the basic aptitude or personality for it, or forget it. I say it's 90% science, 10% art. I've trained many shy, introverted people who came in saying, "I don't have what it takes."

What it takes to be successful at fund raising are two things: genuine passion for your cause and an airtight system. The Raising More Money programs were designed to reconnect people to their passion and then provide the system. They are designed for organizations committed to growing and cultivating a base of lifelong donors.

If you are reading this book, you undoubtedly have at least one nonprofit organization in your life that you love. At some point in the fund-raising process, you have probably had the thought: There must be a better way to do this.

This book is written for staff, board members and volunteers who are passionate about the mission of the organization but burned out on the old model of raising funds. It is for people who are serious about having their organization get off the tread-mill of grant writing and one-year-at-a-time special events and step into the new reality. It is for people who are committed to leaving their favorite nonprofit the legacy of a system of mul-tiple-year pledges for unrestricted operating money—all with an eye to growing a stronger base of lifelong major donors, a capital campaign, endowment or planned giving program.

But be warned: this model takes work and, without a step-by-step guide to its implementation, it can wreak havoc with your current ways of operating. On the brighter side, most people say once they get the hang of it, the Raising More Money approach takes a lot less work than all the "fund raising fluff" they have been suffering over. At least now they see that they are building something for the future: a legacy they could be proud of leaving, a system that is consistent with the new paradigm.

As you read on, consider the possibility that your reading this book could be the cause of the fund-raising breakthrough that your organization so clearly needs. It could be the cause of a breakthrough so complete and so lasting, that 20 years from now, when you come back to visit, you won't even have to ask people why there is no more suffering about the money. You will just be smiling.

CHAPTER 1

ARE YOU READY FOR A
BREAKTHROUGH?

What is a breakthrough, anyway? Is it just another over-worn buzz word? How does it apply to fund raising? What does it really mean?

Think of a breakthrough as a break in your old reality—the reality that is so familiar you do not even notice it. The reality of grant writing, special events, mailings, making your goal one year at a time, drowning in detail that often seems to have nothing to do with the extraordinary mission of your organization and your reason for signing on in the first place.

What if it didn't have to be that way? What if you could break through to a whole new level of stability in your organization's funding? What if you could leave a legacy of a self-generating system for building lifelong donors? What if you could leave the legacy of an endowment fund large enough to cover your annual operating shortfall from its earnings alone? Would that be a legacy worth leaving?

Before you plunge idealistically into the chapters that follow, it is well worth reflecting on whether you are truly ready for such a breakthrough. Ask yourself these questions:

1

What am I committed to having for my organization or program, even though I have no idea how *to make it happen?*

Never mind what the board or the boss would say, what is the hot button for you? Maybe it is getting the funding for the new school building so you can see the smiles on the faces of the kids when they see their new lockers. Maybe it is fully funding an endowment that would provide stability for your most essential program, the one that is constantly teetering on the brink of extinction. Maybe it is fixing the roof or buying a new van or increasing salaries or adding staff or expanding your programs to more people or a broader geographic area.

Whatever it is, large or small, it has to be something *you* are genuinely passionate about—even though you probably have no idea how to make it happen. All you have to know is that it is what you want. Your answer may be something others in your organization have not noticed, or it may be something that is not at the top of their priority list. And if it is something they want too, it still may seem too far out of reach for them to even dream of.

To answer this question, you have to look back to the starry-eyed vision you had when you first took on this position, when fulfilling the mission of this organization seemed doable, before reality set in. Remember back to the time when you were incensed at the thought of kids being bounced between foster homes for so many years until they were legally adopted? Or when the importance of art in each person's everyday life seemed so vital to you? Or when you believed people were smart enough and committed enough to do what it takes to change public policy?

Let yourself indulge in those dreams again for a moment, and then ask yourself: What am I committed to having for this organization even though I may have no idea how to make it happen? What is your answer?

If money were no object, what would be the right thing to spend our money on next?

Notice the question begins, "If money were no object." Most people working with nonprofit organizations today cannot even hear that phrase. "What do you mean, money is no object?" they ask. "Of course it is an object—a limit, a barrier, a hurdle, a brick wall to be overcome. It is the largest barrier we face."

A few years ago, after asking this question in one of our workshops, a participant stayed late to talk. She said, "When you asked us that question, no one could really relate to it. I know because I used to feel like that."

She went on to tell me her story: She had been working in the nonprofit sector for more than 20 years. For the past three years, she had been the executive director of a large family service organization started by three families more than 100 years ago. Back then, it was an orphanage. Over time, the original members of the three families had passed away, as had their successive generations of children, each leaving generous bequests to the organization. They now had an endowment fund of more than $100 million.

This capable executive director no longer had to worry about grant requests and funding cutbacks. Her entire operating budget was funded from the earnings of the endowment fund created by the founding families and others. She no longer had to start each year scrambling to prioritize essential programs based on limited resources.

"Instead," she said, "the board and staff and I have the luxury of waking up each day and asking only one question: What do our children need? What's the right next thing for us to be doing for the children?"

If you're interested in having a breakthrough, you need to answer this question: If money were no object, what would I really want for this organization? What would be the right next thing for us to be spending our money on? Let yourself dream beyond the day-to-day financial limits you have now. The answers will be obvious.

If you knew this was going to be your last year with your organization, what would you want to have happen before you would feel good about turning over your job and walking away?

I'm not suggesting that you leave your organization. Yet, I am often approached by founders, executive directors, and other dedicated staff and volunteers, who confide they feel trapped and embarrassed by the hand-to-mouth nature of their organization's finances. They would be too humiliated to walk away now, leaving their beloved organization in such an unstable financial position.

I suggest you ask yourself this question often. It is designed to help you prioritize and to focus on what really matters to you, on what you intend to accomplish while you are at the helm.

What is that one project or needed area you would want to get up and running before you leave? What is the one thing that would give the organization the stability you want it to have? What is the one thing you may never be remembered for, yet in your own mind, you feel is the thing that is most needed and will not happen if you don't make it happen? What is the one thing that stirs you in the middle of the night or that annoys you because no one else is doing anything about it?

Has it ever occurred to you that maybe you are the one who needs to tackle it, particularly if it seems impossible? If you are passionate enough about why it is needed, then it is the right one to go for. It could be finally building that new building everyone has been talking about, expanding a major program, establishing more equitable compensation for staff, bringing in 100 more major donors, or setting up an endowment or a system for ongoing fund raising.

You name it. This is called the legacy question. Ask it often. Then live as if this will be your last year with your organization. Accomplish that goal, and then you can set the next one.

If twenty years from now you came back to visit your organization and noticed there was no more suffering about raising annual operating funds—the organization had more than enough money to fund its needs—what is the breakthrough that would have happened to produce the abundance of funds?

First, stop for a moment and imagine that this is possible. Imagine that the culture of scarcity and survival in your organization is gone. Money is not an object. The only object is fulfilling the mission. Only one or two people on the staff can even remember the good old days of never having enough money, and even they cannot relate to the suffering you went through back then.

Certainly that would be a breakthrough, an entirely different frame of reference where money is not the limitation. In the new reality, the organizations that will survive will be those that figure out how to produce such a breakthrough. The others will be merged, subsumed or just melt away.

What would have to have happened to produce that breakthrough? For some organizations, the answer will be having a consistent, reliable *system* in place that brings in funds year after year, whether it is a specially-designed, multiple-year individual giving program, or a sustaining endowment fund. For others, it will be having the good work of the organization widely known and respected in the community.

One thing is certain: the breakthrough will involve individuals, lots of individuals, in very tailored, personal ways. The breakthrough will engage and re-engage those individuals in your organization's mission, spell out the needs of the population served, and ask for substantial gifts over multiple years—gifts of a magnitude equal to both the commitment level and giving capacity of the individual donor.

Now, having considered the above questions, what is the breakthrough you are committed to producing for your organization?

What is your vision of the new reality that is big enough and compelling enough to get you through each day, to make it worth doing the work you will need to do to tailor this model to your situation? What is the one thing that, if it were to happen, there would be no way of denying a breakthrough had taken place?

Your answer may be a specific amount of money, or it may not be money at all. Here is how you will know you have arrived at your desired breakthrough. Just saying it out loud will evoke equal amounts of terror and excitement. You will want the breakthrough more than ever, yet still have no idea how to make it happen.

Now you are ready to begin the game of making the impossible happen.

CHAPTER 2

THE LANDSCAPE
OF THE
NEW REALITY

You don't have to look back very far to find the old reality of fund raising. Twenty or thirty years ago will do. If you have been involved in the nonprofit world during that time, whether you like it or not, you have been fully immersed in the old reality.

The most fundamental principle of the old reality was that there were not enough resources to do what needed to be done, and there never would be enough. The needs would always be greater than the available resources.

When the old reality began many years earlier, this was true. If you had taken all the available surplus resources (today we would say capital) and divided them among all the needy projects and people, there would not have been enough to go around. We didn't wonder whether or not there was enough. It was assumed there would always be a scarcity of whatever resources we needed to fix the problem.

We didn't speak much about this insufficiency. It wasn't bad or good. In this reality, scarcity was appropriate. Our thinking and behavior were perfectly consistent with the way we saw and understood the world. It was so much a part of the fabric of life in the nonprofit world, we just took it for granted.

The most obvious source of this thinking in the 20th century was the Depression of the 1930s. Whether we lived through it personally or inherited the thinking of our parents and grand-parents, most of us born in the 40s, 50s, and even the early 60s, got a moderate to heavy dose of this reality. We have been well steeped in "there is not enough."

Somewhere along the way, things began to shift. More people moved into the middle class and began to accumulate economic wealth. The information age was upon us. All that hard work and scrimping began to pay off. Lives that our parents never dreamed of were now possible for relatively ordinary people.

Owning a color television was nothing special. Likewise, two-car families, regular family vacations, and college education became the standard. There often was even enough surplus to invest in quality-of-life issues such as continuing education, physical fitness, environmental concerns, recreation, and the arts.

Fast forward to today and the same member of the Baby Boom generation born to Depression-era parents. There is a microwave in the kitchen, probably more than one phone line for those fax machines, computers and email accounts. And that is just at home. I wrote part of this book on a remote beach in Tahiti under a thatched roof, pecking away at my laptop. When I finished a chapter, I could send it to the editor and download my email.

Try explaining this reality to the folks 30 years ago. The world we inhabit now was unthinkable then. No one could have imagined it. Those were the days when Crayola crayons came in boxes of eight, when three television networks were standard fare, the family car was a Ford or Chevrolet, and either Tide or Cheer could do the job.

This is not meant to be an exercise in nostalgia. The point is that many of us remember that reality as if it were yesterday. Though we would never dream of living our personal lives as if the old reality still prevailed, we are still running our nonprofit organizations that way. We operate from the same scrimping and saving mentality as if we are limited by the same scarce resources.

Scarcity versus Abundance

If the old reality was based on scarcity and survival, the new reality is based on abundance.

The great majority of us have more—and some of us have a lot more. Granted, living in Seattle and spending a fair amount of time in Silicon Valley, my perspective may be a bit skewed. Both regions have been turning out youthful techno-millionaires for several years.

While this concentration of wealth may not be as prevalent in the rest of country, the vast majority of Americans do have more. They are putting more and more of their surplus into investments, planning for retirement, playing (and winning at) the stock market. All the economic indicators are up.

Now let's look at charitable giving.

In 1998, Americans gave nearly $175 billion to charitable organizations, according to *Giving USA*. That is a respectable sum. Of that $175 billion, 85% was given by individuals. Roughly five percent came from corporations and ten percent from foundations.

And the dollar amount contributed by individuals will only go up. Some observers say we are still seeing only the tip of the iceberg.

More and more of the newly affluent, in addition to the wealthy and super-wealthy, have established family foundations and other tax-favored vehicles with specified levels of annual giving. They have institutionalized their giving.

Retired investment manager, Claude Rosenberg, in *Wealthy and Wise—How You and America Can Get the Most Out of Your Giving*, says donations from individuals could easily increase by

$100 billion a year. He contends it is time people start breaking the most sacred of financial rules: Don't spend the principal. Following his carefully-crafted guidelines, he argues, donors can give more without altering their lifestyles and all the while increasing their personal wealth.

And what about that three trillion dollar transfer of wealth we have been hearing about in the inevitable bequeathing of fortunes to the children, grandchildren and great-grandchildren of the wealthy? People are waking up to the fact that they can't take it with them. They are realizing that they will either be leaving it to their families, to their favorite charitable organization, or to taxes.

More and more affluent folks are hearing this news from their financial advisors. Many of them are in their 20's and 30's, and realize they already have more than they will ever need. They are not interested in amassing infinite piles of stuff in their lives or leaving their children trust-fund addicted. They have solid, hard-working, Puritan values, along with a heavy need to give back.

Let me share one of my favorite donor stories:

A friend who works at Microsoft called me from his office one morning. "I just have to tell you about this," he starts off. "You know how much I love Organization X. They do incredible work internationally to end poverty and hunger. They leverage every dollar to the maximum. Their overhead is under two percent. Their total budget for the year, to do all they do, is only $1 million.

"Last night was their annual fund raising dinner here in Seattle. Their goal was to raise $100,000, or ten percent of their whole budget. They succeeded. They were ecstatic.

"I'm still upset about it," he went on, "that they were happy to settle for so little. I love that organization. If they had even thought to ask me, I'd have funded their whole budget for the year.

"Then I think to myself," he continues, "I'm sitting here right now on the Microsoft campus, looking out at all these people. So many of these people could have funded this organization several times over, or for that matter, funded *their* favorite charity many times over or fully funded that organization's endowment. But no one's asking us!"

We will talk more in a later chapter about the demographics of today's donors. For now, the point to be made is how much money is out there and how many people are looking for a worthy place to contribute that money. I could recount endless stories of donors asking in their own way: "How do I give these days? How do I connect with a charitable organization that would want what I have to offer? Why don't they ever ask me for more?"

They are looking for organizations that have stepped into the new reality and can relate to them on their own level. They want to hear your passion about your work. They want to hear your stories and testimonials about how your work changes lives. They want to know the facts about the problem and your organization's success in solving it. They want to understand the gap between where you are now and what it would take to fulfill your mission. You have to make that gap crystal clear. Then they will want to hear your plan and how they can be part of fulfilling it.

What they don't want to hear is your poor, sad story of woe and suffering. That is a vestige of some reality they are not familiar with. It falls on deaf ears. It will not resonate with them. It will send them on their way to find another organization that speaks their language—the language of abundance and plenty. The language of "it can be done" and "it will be done." These are can-do donors who want to be part of a solution. They are doing their research before making their investment. They want to be sure they are picking a winner.

The organizations that recognize that the new reality is paved with abundant resources and generous people wanting to contribute will be the organizations that will thrive. Will yours be among them?

Your Money Baggage

You might want to notice, before we move on, your own discomfort with this topic. All this abundance talk is likely to sound a little too "new age." You might consider that maybe, just maybe, you are clinging to a residual strain of the old reality, that world of suffering and scarcity that feels so much more familiar and comfortable.

When I first began offering the Raising More Money workshop, I brought in a remarkable "new reality" financial planner, Karen Ramsey, author of *Everything You Know About Money is Wrong: Overcoming the Financial Myths Keeping You From the Life You Want* to work with participants to discover their basic issues about money.

The poignancy was not lost on any of us. One by one, using a carefully-crafted series of non-threatening questions, Karen elicited from each person the underlying "money message" that pretty much ran the show for them. For some it was: "I don't deserve it." For others it was, "There's never enough." "Money is evil," was another popular one.

The exercise was useful for many reasons. First, we were all surprised at the number of people working in the fund development field who had backgrounds of substantial wealth. Some had even hidden their identities or changed their names to remain anonymous.

The second surprise was the heavy baggage we all carry about money. Whichever side of the fund-raising fence we sit on, asker or donor, our issues about money keep us firmly implanted in the old reality. It is a wonder people actually get beyond their fear of asking or their fear of being manipulated and taken advantage of in giving. Fund raising is fraught with emotional baggage, all of it a vestige of the old reality.

Third, it is possible to get beyond these issues. In less than 30 minutes, Karen's laser-like skill had each of us reduced to our own one-line platitude that rang so true it hurt. There is something about knowing what that one essential phrase is that forever after alerts you when your particular issue begins to run the show.

Imagine it is an hour before your big "Ask" with your major potential donor. She has already become personally involved and given you all the signals she is ready to make her first major gift to your organization. As much as you love your organization and as much as you know she wants to give, you don't know how you will bring yourself to "make the Ask." Or perhaps asking her for a gift doesn't scare you; your worry is berating yourself afterwards for not getting a big enough gift. (We call that "asker's remorse.") What would get in the way at those moments? If you could get your "money baggage" out of the way, you would be fearless and free to ask in the terms of the new reality.

But stepping into the new reality will not necessarily look like a good idea at first. Even if you are armed with all the statistics about donors today, clinging to the old familiar way will certainly seem smarter.

You Must Have a System

It seems pretty obvious, when viewed inside that old reality thinking, we should be thankful for whatever we can get.

Here we are, the poor, long-suffering nonprofit organization, working on behalf of our particular cause, wishing and hoping for a handout. In the old reality, to put it crassly, we were pitiful beggars. If we were courageous (or desperate) enough to hold our hand out, we were grateful for whatever we got.

Twenty-five dollars? One hundred dollars? Whatever we were fortunate enough to get, we appreciated. That was consistent with the unspoken commitment of the old-reality, nonprofit culture—suffer the scarcity of resources nobly.

What that mentality got us was a year-to-year, hand-to-mouth existence, a poverty mentality that begat poverty and kept us on the scarcity treadmill. We weren't even bothered by it. It was part of the mantle of working in the nonprofit world. You were supposed to be accustomed to having it be that way.

Furthermore, it was a haphazard, shotgun approach, based on our needs of the moment. The most forward-looking we got was thinking about next year's annual event or annual campaign. Except in the largest, most established institutions, no conscious thought was given to a self-sustaining system. It was pretty much hand-to-hand combat, eking out an existence one year at a time. And as with everything else in the old reality, this was all given. Very few thought to question it.

When held up against the template of the new reality, this way of thinking seems almost pathetic. Not only does it dishonor your work by presuming no one would think it essential enough to fund long-term, it insults your donors as well.

Perhaps that statement is a bit strong, but, as with the rest of this book, it is meant to be a wake-up call.

In the new reality, you must have a *system*—a system for building and growing your self-sustaining individual giving program, a custom-designed machine that manages you. It tells you, "Oops, it's been three months since anyone has talked to those first-time donors. What is their preferred medium? Phone, mail, online? What is the next level of engagement you would want their permission for? If you were treating this first-time donor of $25 as someone who will become a lifelong major donor, what more would you want to know about them? How can you engage them in precisely the ways they would like to be engaged?"

To be a true, self-sustaining system, by definition it wouldn't need you to keep reminding it to do its thing. *It* would remind *you*. There would be built-in tickler points that would ask just the right questions. Your answers, when customized to that particular donor, would steer the system to the next appropriate form of contact.

Anything short of an airtight system will leave you back in the old hand-to-mouth reality: suffering.

Leaving the Legacy of an Endowment

Here is another new-reality zinger: If your organization has been around longer than 10 years, you should have an endowment fund large enough to fully fund your operating shortfall every year, just from its earnings.

You see, in the new reality, your old suffering routine looks like whining. If your mission is so great, if that work is so important, why are you being so stingy with it? Why, if you have given *your* life to it, and if you have donors who truly believe in its value, would you hold back on spinning the big vision? Why would you hold back on letting them know what it would take to handle the whole problem? Are you assuming they couldn't take the bad news? Or that you would be found out for not knowing the perfect solution?

Consider for a moment that perhaps your donors are the key to the solution, to the fulfillment of your mission. Maybe they are the missing piece in the puzzle that will actually cure the dreaded disease or locate the essential ingredient you have only dreamed of.

Consider that perhaps you are holding back on being honest and forthright with your donors in favor of the old reality: suffering. Have you ever had the thought that maybe you are the one in the way of the solution, that maybe, rather than being the savior for your cause, you have become part of the problem?

Since odds are your mission will never be fulfilled without more people getting on board with you, I recommend you step into the new reality and let these loyal supporters contribute more fully whatever they have to contribute. In many cases it will be their money.

In the new reality, you will see donors coming forward to seed endowments for their favorite organizations. They will shepherd them for several years or a lifetime until they are fully funded. They may do this for several organizations. It is the kind of legacy they want to leave.

The only thing missing is the visionary leader who can paint a compelling picture of a world in which the mission of the organization is fulfilled. That leader will need to quantify the gaping chasm between the state of the problem today and what it will take to accomplish a solution. Exactly what is your best guess at what it will take? Tell them that.

Say your program is only reaching 20% of the abused children in your region. What would it cost to reach them all? Another $3 million a year? And how much money would you need to have invested in an endowment fund so the interest from the endowment would equal or exceed $3 million annually?

Most nonprofit folks can barely hear this question. The number seems impossible, huge, unthinkable! They can hardly imagine reaching their goal for this year, let alone expanding their services to all those in need. An endowment sounds positively greedy!

Precisely the point. That insidious, old-reality, hand-to-mouth suffering mentality does not die easily, and if you let it, it will win out every time.

Just do the math, quantify the gap and endow it. What is your number? Start thinking about that number as you read the stock market reports, as you read about all those folks making more and more money. Then think about your existing loyal supporters who could help to make this happen. Start talking about an endowment.

Today's donors don't want to hear your sad story. They want to hear your plan. Tell them the facts as simply and directly as you can (and spare them the sugar coating). Let them in on all the passion you suppress everyday; your fears and uncertainties, where you feel you are losing ground. Share what it is that keeps you going. They will want to fund that. They can take it.

It is time for nonprofit organizations to grow up about money. It is like being a young child barely making it through half the week before your allowance is spent. By college, you can make it through three-quarters of the month. As a young adult, you are actually able to make it paycheck to paycheck, plus a modest credit card debt. As you start to earn more, you take on more debt. One day you wake up and realize nobody else is going to bale you out. Not only do *you* have to pay off those debts, someone has to start funding that retirement account. The earnings off that account will need to equal your annual cost of living.

Suddenly you are thinking differently. You handle your debt and start saving more. If you were smart enough to wake up early enough, you will be okay and have that retirement funded. But it usually takes a wake-up call to change your thinking.

What is the legacy you want to leave for your organization? You are not going to be there forever. Other than curing that disease or completely fulfilling your organization's mission, your next-best legacy will be leaving an endowment.

The donors are waiting. In many cases, they may be wondering what is taking you so long to put your plan together and ask for their support.

CHAPTER 3

A CUSTOMIZED APPROACH TO REACHING AND KEEPING LIFELONG DONORS

In the old reality, we could get by just fine without having to raise money from individuals. There seemed to be enough to make ends meet with government funding, a relatively stable pattern of United Way funding, and grants from private foundations and corporations. Whatever funds you were able to raise from individuals were considered "gravy." Special events and direct-mail programs, even the annual campaign, were never relied upon as the major sources of funding.

The old reality said: Other than government grants or fees paid by clients or theatergoers for tickets, nonprofit organizations should focus on raising money from foundations and corporations whose guidelines are known rather than focusing on the slow, time-intensive process of courting individual donors.

In the new reality, individual donors will be the centerpiece of your fund-raising strategy. Organizations without a strong base of individual support will fade away. Those organizations with a system for building and cultivating lifelong donors—donors who understand and feel connected to the work of the organization—will thrive.

When I meet with an organization for the first time and ask them what they are already doing to raise money, they invariably say they are writing proposals for grant funding. In many cases, they have a full-time grant proposal writer, sometimes more than one. When I ask how much the organization raised from grants in the prior year, there is often a pause and then some uncertainty about the real number.

In the old reality, dependence on government and private grant-funding was presumed, welcomed, and appreciated. In fact, the more savvy you were about how to play the grantsmanship game and win, the more your nonprofit peers envied you. You knew how to research all the funding organizations and their funding priorities for the year. You knew how to creatively turn your basic operating needs into their hot-topic packages, using just the right buzz-words to get your grant request funded.

Once the grant was awarded, you would never dream of letting a full year pass without some contact. You would invite them back for a show-and-tell event, send them letters and reports on what their money was providing. In other words, you would take really good care of them. These same methods for being successful with foundations, corporations, and in some cases, government funders, are what it will take to be successful with individuals today.

Why focus on individuals?

Stop to let the facts sink in. In the new reality, 85% of the money contributed to nonprofit organizations comes from individuals. Only 5% comes from corporations and 10% from foundations. Those ratios indicate that if you have one full-time grant proposal writer, you ought to have seven or eight full-time staff working on individual giving. How does your organization stack up?

Here are the major pitfalls of grant dependence; see if they sound familiar:

First, if you are successful raising money from grants, it is probably because, at least in part, you have a personal relationship with the grant makers. You know them by name. They know your organization by name. The only problem is that in most cases the person you are dealing with is an intermediary to the person or people with the money. Rarely will you ever deal with the ultimate decision maker. The intermediary reports to a committee. The committee has "guidelines" for giving. Over time, those guidelines change. While your organization might fall within those guidelines this year, odds are that three or four years down the road your cause will have lost its appeal and they will move on to another cause.

In all fairness to foundations and corporations, this is entirely their prerogative. They don't exist to make you happy. They exist to fulfill on the giving priorities of their donors. If your organization is receiving a grant of $2,500 per year for three years in a row from the same foundation or corporation, you should consider yourself extremely fortunate.

I recommend you use these years of strong grant funding to build your parallel structure of individual giving. In the new reality, your individual giving program will be the centerpiece of your fund-raising efforts. There are at least three good reasons this is true.

First of all, individual giving is where the money is. That should be obvious by now.

Second, it frees your organization from its dependence on grants, including government grants, and lets you take your future into your own hands. Most organizations live in mortal fear of the day when their one big funding source backs off. Now is the time to be building your parallel system for lifelong individual donors.

Third, developing a strong individual giving program allows you to deal directly with the ultimate decision makers, the donors themselves.

The Value of a Lifelong Donor

Let's look at why it is worth taking the time to make individual giving the centerpiece of your fund-raising program.

Start by thinking about your own giving last year. Make a mental list of the organizations to which you gave money. Was it to the kids selling cookies in front of the grocery store, to your favorite religious organization, to the local public television telethon, or to your alma mater?

For each of those places, think back to how many years in a row you have given to that same organization. If you are like most donors, you have a core group of organizations on your list that have been the fortunate beneficiaries of your loyal support year after year.

Individuals are loyal donors. For whatever reason, we tend to have favorite places to give and we just keep giving there. We may not expect a big thank you or talk about these places with our friends. They are our own private causes or issues, and we feel good about supporting them.

Next, as individuals, *our disposable income generally increases as we get older.* Which is to say, if properly courted, we most likely have the capacity to give more and more.

Finally, as individuals, *we often can give beyond our lifetimes.* Charitable foundations rarely give away the principal of their funds because their mission usually includes staying around to continue giving away a percentage of their interest every year. Individuals, on the other hand, can't take it with them. Ultimately, their assets are either going to their children, to taxes, or to their favorite charity. At some point, most people realize this and get into the driver's seat about estate planning. That should be good news for you—if your individual giving program is ready.

As individual giving becomes the key component of their fund development program, organizations will offer donors many options for capital giving, planned and deferred giving. Giving options will be designed, first and foremost, to meet the needs of donors. Meeting the needs of the organization will be secondary. Corporate and foundation grants will still be sought, but as a minor adjunct to the main system for individual giving.

Mass Marketing versus a Customized Approach

In the old reality, the fundamental principle of scarcity prevailed. There was never enough and there never would be enough. When it came to fund raising, this meant every organization always needed more money. Organizations generally concluded that rather than taking the time get more money from each individual donor, it would be quicker and easier to get more new donors. A mass-marketing, acquire-new-donors-at-any-cost mentality prevailed. We were in a feeding frenzy to find new donors.

In the old reality, the bulge in the population was younger and waiting to be acquired. Much like the younger, high-technology, potential donors today, back then most of us were still "undecided." We were sitting happily in our zip codes waiting for our phones to ring, reading our mail, watching our televisions. There were far fewer demands on our time. If a cause came along that touched our fancy, we gave. It was easy and impersonal; we could just send back that envelope with a check.

In the old reality, no one ever knew exactly what it was about that organization's cause that hooked us as a donor. Did someone we know die from that disease? Did someone we know have that same social need? Had we lived on a farm, near a river or lake? No one ever bothered to ask us why we were giving.

Then, the next month, or the next quarter, the organization was already out looking for new donors. Would previous donors give again? Maybe yes, maybe no. By then, they were hardly the focus of the organization's effort. Fund raising was just an impersonal numbers game. All the incentives were designed to get more new donors with little or no attention paid to why those new donors gave in the first place.

Nor did we care if they stopped giving in the next month or year. As long as our net number of donors was increasing, we were winning at the game. It was the basic mass marketing approach of the old reality. Donors were just an anonymous bundle of demographics with a checkbook.

In the old reality, we presumed a great deal. We were bold enough to presume we knew the kind of donors we wanted. We knew where they lived, the kinds of cars they drove, where their kids went to school. If we were looking for new donors, we could safely presume that five people living on the same block, driving pretty much the same car, were pretty much the same—at least in terms of their purchasing patterns and in terms of their beliefs. We actually were audacious enough to think we knew you.

In the old reality, we could get away with those kinds of assumptions because the "products" we were offering you were equally plain vanilla. Whether we were asking for $5 or $10 to support the good work of an organization or for your old household castoffs, the giving options were conveniently limited so we didn't need to know much more about you than the basics.

About the only reason for knowing demographic information at all was for direct-mail solicitation. This was done by professional direct-mail companies, often at a fairly high cost. Their coverage was broad enough to allow for large margins of error. If you were looking to get new, first-time donors using direct mail or telemarketing, you were prepared to pay dearly for the mass marketing approach. You knew that for every hundred people in the same neighborhood with the same type of car and income, only a certain percentage would return their response envelope with a check. Yet back then, we were satisfied with return rates of 2 to 3%. We didn't need to care about what the other 97% thought. If we cast the net widely enough, we would get enough fish for our dinner.

Ridiculous as that approach may seem in the new reality, the vast majority of nonprofit organizations continue it to this day. In the new reality, however, an acquisition-centered strategy is not going to yield as much. That is because, in the new reality, there just aren't as many hungry fish out there. In fact, most of the Baby Boomers making up the largest "bulge" in the population today have already been acquired. That is not to say they can't be tempted to add another charity to their giving list. But given the tremendous loyalty of individual donors to their core group of charities, all of that mass marketing expense for the sole purpose of acquisition seems wasteful.

Every smart, new-reality marketing expert will tell you that it costs at least five times more to acquire a new donor than it does to renew and upgrade an existing donor. In other words, there is absolutely no point in having a fancy donor acquisition program without also having a conscious plan for renewing and upgrading donors on an ongoing basis. The direct-mail companies will be the first to tell you that you need to start "skimming off" the names of the repeat or high-end donors and getting to know them. Most direct-mail firms have now developed fairly sophisticated personalization mechanisms to enable you to customize your approach to each donor.

Yet, unless this customized approach engages the donor in a true give-and-take dialog, the entire process will still seem to the donor like a one-way street. To them, this is just more of the old reality: Wonderful Organization X is out begging again. You haven't entered into the new reality until you have developed an automatic system that insures ongoing, personal dialog being done on a one-on-one basis, either over the telephone, online, or—ideally—in person.

Imagine for a moment you already have all the donors you will ever need? What if, instead of the perpetual obsession with the expensive, yet less scary, direct-mail acquisition approach, you decided to focus on getting to know the donors you already have? What if your emphasis was on how to deepen your relationship with each donor in a highly personalized system that transforms them from a one-time or occasional donor to a lifelong advocate and insider? What could that approach yield? Suddenly, that mass marketing approach seems stale and obsolete.

A Customized Dialog

The old reality assumed donors were all the same. In the new reality we go out of our way at every opportunity to *ask* you how you are unique. We assume nothing. We ask and keep asking. We track your preferences and actions and adjust accordingly. The next time we talk to you, we have incorporated what you said you liked. After each significant interaction, we ask for your feedback again. We continually customize our interactions with you based on what you tell us.

As soon as you begin to engage the donor in this type of dialog, you will have stepped into the new reality. You will have begun a donor-directed, one-step-at-a-time, interactive program for a happy, lifelong donor.

We have become accustomed to this in our personal lives. For example, we order a computer online by selecting the exact specifications we want, having it custom-made and delivered within a week. Or we order groceries online for home delivery. The next time we place an order, the screen shows us a pared down list of our preferences—no meat for vegetarians, low fat only, etc. We return to a business hotel where we are greeted by name and given our preferred room type and morning newspaper without being asked.

Many of us have come to expect this type of customization in our personal lives without even realizing it. Yet most non-profit organizations are still operating back in the old reality of mass marketing and blindly generalizing about our donors' preferences. Rather than asking 100 people we presume to be similar to our donors about their preferences and then generalizing, we need to ask those very donors or potential donors themselves, not their surrogates or some computer model of "those kinds" of people.

In the new reality, organizations need a system for repeatedly gathering this vital, customized input and tailoring their approach to each donor based on ongoing, personal feedback. The new reality calls for a willingness to listen to our donors, to respect their wishes, to act in concert with their level of comfort or trust in our organization, to let the relationship unfold at their pace.

This customized approach to individual donors requires a major shift in our thinking. While in theory it sounds like a good idea, seeking out and welcoming feedback does not always come easily to nonprofit organizations.

In my work at Zion Preparatory Academy, a remarkable private school for inner-city youth in Seattle, input and feedback from everyone in the community was always welcomed. Fortunately, the leadership of the school was certain enough of its philosophical underpinnings that they were not threatened or put off every time a donor came along with another good idea for a special program or a new way to educate the children. Rather than shun this input, the principal, Doug Wheeler, welcomed the dialog as a chance to learn from the donors and to educate them about the approach he was committed to following.

This type of open dialog with your donors and volunteers is no longer optional. In the new reality, it is essential to keeping your organization fresh and vital. It is essential to building the kind of lifelong donors you are looking for. To operate effectively in the new reality you must actually want to know what your donors and volunteers think. You must have an appreciation for their opinions. You must know where you stand on the core issues that affect the work of your organization.

The donors who truly understand your mission and are as passionate about it as you are, those are the donors of the new reality. They want a good debate once in awhile. They want you to hear them out. They want to be educated by the dialog; they want to come away having learned more about the issue. Rather than scare them away, this level of communication will deepen their commitment to your work. In turn, you need to be open to what your organization stands to gain from the dialog. Those organizations that willingly embrace, and truly enjoy this interactive, personalized approach will be the ones that thrive in the new reality.

CHAPTER 4

THE "IDEAL" DONOR VERSUS THE DONOR NEXT DOOR

Let's look at the old-reality stereotype of the "ideal" donor versus the reality of today's donors.

In the old reality, if we spent any time at all raising money from individuals, we probably had a basic stereotype of our ideal donor. He was an older, white, wealthy male. Of course, we would have been happy with any new donor we could get, but we knew the donors with the potential to become serious major donors were the ones who fit our stereotype.

This stereotype of the ideal donor correlated perfectly with our old-reality system of asking. As we will discuss in Chapter 6, this was the peer-to-peer, "strong-arm-thy-Rolodex" approach to asking. That method worked back then. We had one type of target donor in mind. We knew where to find him and who should ask him so he couldn't say no. It was a neat, tight little asking system.

Thankfully, we can say goodbye to that reality.

In the new reality, everyone is a potential donor and a potential major donor. When you look at the statistics, you begin to see why it is time to shift our image of the ideal donor from the older white male to the "donor next door".

Here is the first statistic to let sink in: At least one person in over 70% of American households donates to charity. That means nearly three out of four of us, perhaps more, gives money in the course of a year. No need to wonder where to find these donors; they are everywhere. No need to wait around for Bill Gates; that $150 billion from individuals comes from all of us. We are a country of givers.

In the new reality, the American dream will be to become a philanthropist. More and more, the reason people will want to make more money is so they can give it away. Regardless of their age, ethnicity or socio-economic background, happily, our world will be filled with more people like Matel "Mat" Dawson:

> DETROIT - Matel "Mat" Dawson has worked for the Ford Motor Co. for 59 years and could have retired long ago. But the 78-year-old is still at it, driving a forklift, soaking up as much overtime as possible and pulling down around $100,000 a year.
>
> Just so he can give most of it away.
>
> With a $200,000 donation to Wayne State University yesterday, Dawson has now donated more than $1 million to schools and charities since 1994.
>
> "I get joy, happiness out of this," he said at a news conference, nattily dressed in a pin-stripe suit with a pink boutonniere. "I can go home and sleep good."
>
> *Seattle Post Intelligencer, April 14, 1999*

Ethnic Diversity

In contrast to the ideal donor in the old reality, the donor next door of the new reality will more closely mirror the demographics of today's communities. As more of our diverse society moves up the economic ranks, so, too, will their giving increase. Whether Caucasian, African-American, Hispanic, Asian, gay or lesbian, youth or retiree, the key predictors of giving will be the same.

Predictors of Giving

These two predictors have remained reliable over time: education level and household income. A recent study by Independent Sector, which closely monitors trends in giving and volunteering over time, once again found that "as the level of education and household income increased, so did both the volunteering and contributing rate."

An additional predictor of individual giving which cuts across all lines, seems ridiculously obvious. In the same study, a full 81 percent of households surveyed said the key impetus in their giving was simply *being asked*. Furthermore, "respondents who were asked to give by someone they knew well were twice as likely to contribute if they were asked than if they were not."

Age

In the old reality, the ideal major donor had matured to a point in his career where he could afford to begin to give some of his accumulated wealth away. In other words, the stereotypical major donor had probably reached the prime of his career and was at least age 50.

In the new reality, the age of the major donor next door could be nearly any age from cradle to grave. From trust-fund babies to teenage philanthropists to retired 20- and 30- something techno-millionaires, there is pretty much no telling anymore what age your major donors could be.

Pay close attention to those elementary school kids organizing classroom community service projects and those teenagers running their own school or community-based foundations. Let go of your stereotypes of what age your donors will be, what they will look like, what clothes they will wear, where they will live.

The safest bet is to just assume you don't have a clue. In other words, treat everyone you come in contact with as if they are or could be the biggest and best donor you have ever had.

Gender

There is one more stereotype that must be put to rest in the new reality. The old reality assumed (and often for good reason) the man made the money and was in charge of giving it away. Including the woman in the process was merely a courtesy.

In the new reality, the majority of donors will be women. Whether attributed to their longevity, their "giving" nature, or their earning power, every new reality individual giving program will need to place a major emphasis on cultivating women as lifelong donors.

Noted fund raising demographer Judith Nichols, in her book *Global Demographics*, cites the following five reasons "for seriously targeting women for your organization's fund-raising efforts":

- Women have increasing economic power.
- Women tend to save more of their incomes than do men. They are more attuned, at an earlier age, to concerns about outliving assets, making them prime candidates for planned gifts.
- Women outlive men, controlling the disposition of their own estates and, often, that of the spouse as well.
- Women have a new awareness of the power of the dollars they control. They are choosing charities that reflect their concerns and interests.
- Women are more charitably inclined than men. They make three times the number of donations as do males. Women leave more bequests to charity than do men.

Tune in to women's preferred style of giving. They want to be more involved. They want to see first-hand how their gift will make a difference.

Pay attention to how much time you are focusing on the man as the potential major donor. In the new reality, in the majority of cases, the woman will be the decision maker about charitable giving. Include the spouse or female partner wherever possible. In some cases, a daughter or sister may need to be included in the cultivation process as well.

A participant in one of our Raising More Money workshops, the Director of Development at a major national arts organization, told me this story. He was busy cultivating Mr. CEO, because his wife was a known arts lover. Each call to the CEO was screened by his assistant, a mere "secretary." It took a few months of personal interaction with the secretary for this savvy development director to pick up on the hints. This secretary was herself an heir to a large fortune and her passion in life was art. Thanks to careful listening, this woman became a lifelong major donor, and she, in turn, helped to cultivate her "boss" as a major donor as well.

Women also will remember how they were treated by your organization. New-reality women donors will have no tolerance for a patronizing approach. Seek out and develop lifelong relationships with women donors in their own right. Treat every woman as a potential major donor.

Personal Connection

Whether they start off with their penny jar or a trust-fund disbursement check, each and every one of those 70% of Americans who give could become, at some point in their lives, a major donor to a charitable organization. Will it be yours?

While their first gift may be for purely emotional reasons or in response to being "strong-armed" by a friend, what it will take to transform them into a lifelong donor is a feeling of personal connection with the organization.

Most donors are wondering what size gift they need to give for your organization to notice them. Will it take many gifts of smaller amounts, month after month, year after year? Or will it take one large gift? If so, how large?

They are looking for a connection that may not require much time. They want to know that you know them as a human being distinct from the next donor. You know what interests them, uniquely, about your work. You know their preferences, their hot buttons, enough to know what it would take to deepen their commitment to your work.

To put it simply, in the new reality, the donors your organization is looking to develop want to talk to you. They want to connect in some more personalized way than receiving a quarterly newsletter. They want to hear, to a greater or lesser extent, about the real issues and challenges the organization is facing as it fulfills its mission.

In turn, they want to know you are interested in them. They need to know that, even in a small way, they are special to you. They need to know that their opinions are valuable to you; that their contacts and unique resources are invaluable to you.

Otherwise, they won't stick around for long. They will take their huge bundle of resources elsewhere—to an organization that will give them that kind of personal contact, customized to their unique needs and personality.

You Are the Donor Next Door

This book is intended to give you a system for building life-long donors, starting with getting to know your existing donors, including a strategy for how to prioritize and where to begin. Moreover, it is designed to stimulate a new way of thinking about how you relate to your individual donors. In essence, you need to be relating to them the same way you'd want to be related to.

In the Raising More Money workshops, we do several exercises to have participants realize that our donors are just like us. They are, for the most part, regular folks, busy with other things in life, yet committed to the work of the organizations they support. While they may not even think about your organization much, something has hooked them enough to give money.

What would it take to have them move to the next level? What would it take to deepen your connection to this early-stage donor who has the potential to become a lifelong major donor?

The sooner you begin to treat your donors as real people, with real concerns and passions, the more successful your program will become.

These donors next door, nearly three-quarters of us, are just regular folks wanting to make a difference with our giving. Remember, every donor has the potential to become a major donor. Be vigilant in monitoring your stereotypes. Don't presume anything. Ask and listen as you gather information about everyone.

Granted, this type of personalized approach is time-consuming. It is also highly effective. Enjoy the unwieldy, interactive process. Enjoy the vibrant dialog. This is what it will take to build lifelong donors in the new reality.

CHAPTER 5

THE NEW
VOLUNTEER

One of the clearest vestiges of the old reality in most non-profit organizations is the volunteer program. It was designed with the best of intentions for the volunteers of yesterday and was a perfect fit for their needs back then.

I remember going to special classes about how to set up and run a volunteer program—how to design the job descriptions, clarify expectations and time limits for the assignment, have a sign-in book with a friendly greeter, a place for the volunteers to chat, have coffee, and have their social needs fulfilled. By all means the program needed to be supervised by a Volunteer Coordinator who knew how to take care of these invaluable people who were giving their time. There were volunteer recognition programs to be put in place, including events and certificates. It was a tight little system designed for the ideal volunteer of the old reality: a woman or retired person who had plenty of extra time on their hands.

One of the main taboos of this system was asking these loyal volunteers to give money. That was a giant "no-no." After all, they were already giving their time and talent. It would be rude to ask them for money. Furthermore, in the old reality, the majority of volunteers were women, who, according to the stereotype, didn't have control over the purse strings anyway. Other than board members, volunteers were never expected to be donors.

Fast forward to the new reality. Think of the places you and your family volunteer right now: Chairing that committee at your religious organization, serving on a committee at your kids' school, helping out for the elections at the local neighborhood association, tutoring at the literacy program.

Notice you have quite a little list. You are not alone. In America, 56% of adults volunteer. This is an increase of nearly 14% in two years. Add to that all the elementary school and youth volunteer programs. Volunteering is no longer just for the wealthy or retired. Today, the majority of us volunteer. It has become part of our culture.

Now look at how much time you give to each of those places you volunteer. It adds up quickly. Three hours a month, six hours a week? I find it remarkable that, in the midst of people's extraordinarily busy lives, giving time—the most precious commodity today—is becoming even more popular. It says a great deal about the sense of meaning and purpose volunteer experiences provide. It also says a great deal about the deeper, more lasting connections people are seeking. More and more of us are turning to volunteer "work" to round out our lives.

Now, go back through your list and rate each of your volunteer experiences in terms of how satisfying it was for you. Tell the truth. The fishing field trip with the inner-city kids might get a 10. Some of the other committee assignments, the ones where you spend much of your time listening to others drone on, may rate only a five.

Think about what could be done to make you a happier volunteer. What annoys you most about each volunteer project or assignment? How could they fix it to make it work better for you? How could they customize it?

In the old reality, the organization called the shots. They said: "We need tutors three days a week; we need candy stripers at 2 p.m." The organization's needs drove the program. That worked pretty well when the primary sources of volunteers were affluent women and retired senior citizens.

In the new reality, "volunteer" takes on a whole new meaning. The edges of "volunteer" blur with the edges of "donor." In the new reality, the organizations that thrive will be those that treat volunteers as lifelong, major donors. And they will treat donors as volunteers.

Volunteer = Donor

The new reality calls for a greatly expanded definition of what it means to be a volunteer for a nonprofit organization. In the new reality, the words "donor" and "volunteer" will be interchangeable. The definition of volunteering will shift from being organization-centered to being volunteer-centered. Rather than recruiting volunteers for pre-set slots, organizations will be asking this new, loosely-defined breed of volunteers how they would like to become involved.

Nothing will look quite the same. "Volunteering" will begin to resemble a series of unrelated projects, dictated by the donor's interest and schedule. From the organization's perspective, it will look like isolated, almost random intersections where donors tell you what they want to do and then do it.

From the donor's perspective, it will feel like a satisfying relationship with you. In their world, when they are at a social gathering and people ask them what they have been doing lately, their "little project" with your organization will figure prominently in their conversation. That is because it will work well for them. Their "volunteer work" will have been customized to their schedule, their interest, and their unique situation.

Let me give you an example. Several years ago, while working full-time and raising two young kids, my husband and I realized we wanted to do more to teach our kids about giving back. At the time, I had been working with organizations that served the homeless. I had found the intractable problem of family homelessness to be very compelling.

I called a local transitional housing program and asked if there would be a way for my family to volunteer. Was there a way we could contribute appropriately to these families? I knew there were confidentiality issues. Yet I was sure there was something they needed that we could provide.

The creative executive director on the other end of the phone saw the opportunity immediately. She knew I was well-meaning, fairly well-connected, and busy. What I was asking for did not fit any neatly-prescribed job description, yet she knew better than to turn down a good resource who could become a long-term supporter.

I asked if perhaps we could put on a party for the residents and families, something appropriate to the season. We were too late. The holiday party was already spoken for.

"How about a birthday party?" I mused. "Most of the kids probably never get a real birthday party—clown and balloons and all."

"Well, how would that work?" she asked with an open mind. "We wouldn't want to exclude any of the kids or families."

What we cooked up was a party for all the kids with birthdays in November. Everyone in the shelter was invited. Early one Saturday morning, my husband, two kids and I, loaded with bags of food, streamers and balloons, took on decorating the room, setting up the party, greeting everyone, serving the food, and introducing the clown. We all had the time of our lives.

Our son, then six years old, was in charge of serving second helpings of ice cream. He walked around the room with a half-dripping carton, quietly stopping at each place and offering more. For him, the most memorable moment was when he ran out of ice cream while serving "thirds" to a little boy about his own age. He came running up to me to ask what to do. "Mom, he wants more and I'm all out. What should I do?"

I handed him a new carton of ice cream and said, "Give him all he wants." I remember watching as the little boy's mother, sitting right beside him, glowed as her son finally became satiated with ice cream! My kids learned more in those few hours than any other classroom could have taught them. Plus, we had an extraordinary experience as a family.

Of course, by the time we had cleaned up the place and were out of there, my husband and I had made the list of 11 other families we were certain would agree to host the birthday party of the month at this shelter. We got their commitments, put the calendar together, and presented the plan to the executive director. How could she refuse? As it happens, one of the other mothers was involved in the Junior League. By the end of the year, the entire project had been adopted as an ongoing Junior League project and it continues to thrive today.

Now, let's dissect the process a bit. First, I spoke to the executive director—someone who was highly entrepreneurial, with natural street-smarts, and with whom I had enough of a past relationship that she knew I was serious.

If instead, I had talked to the volunteer coordinator, assuming she was an old-reality volunteer coordinator, I most likely would have been met with the familiar response, "I'm sorry, we can't let volunteers host parties. It violates the confidentiality of our residents. The jobs we have for volunteers are: playground attendant, dinner server, tutor, etc." There is nothing wrong with any of those jobs. They just weren't what we had in mind.

Just as with donors, today's volunteers need to call the shots. They need to be able to tell you what they want to do, for as much time as they want to do it.

Here is a statistic to consider: *Giving and Volunteering in America* reports that 84% of all the households that contributed to charities in 1998 had at least one volunteer in that household. Furthermore, the dollar amount of contributions from those households was 2.5 times higher than that of non-volunteer households.

So think again. If you have volunteers who are not giving to your organization, the odds are they are giving somewhere else, perhaps to several other organizations. In the new reality, money clearly follows involvement. Where else would people rather give than to the organizations with which they feel most connected? If you are not giving your volunteers an opportunity to contribute, most likely you have still got one foot stuck in the old reality.

Let's look at your trepidation. It is certainly true that some of the "guild ladies" and other hard working, hands-on volunteers might be thoroughly insulted that you would have the nerve to ask them for money. On the other hand, in my experience, if you take the time to ask your volunteers how they would feel about giving money, the majority will tell you they have been wondering what took you so long to ask. The majority will tell you they would be delighted to give.

After all, they are most likely among the three-quarters of Americans who are giving money somewhere. They are giving you their time and their emotional commitment—two gifts which, in today's world, may be more valuable than money. Yet, your organization is holding back on asking them for money for fear of offending them.

Later, in Chapter 22, I will offer a non-threatening, permission-based system for developing a volunteer-led, volunteer-giving program.

Rethinking Your Definition of Volunteer

Here is another example. A friend, age 50, recently retired after selling his business for an eight-figure sum and began looking to get involved with a nonprofit.

"I want to be involved with kids but I don't want to tutor or be a mentor," he tells me. "I wouldn't want a kid to get that dependent on me having to show up at a set time every week. I have another idea. From time to time, I'd like to take kids on outings, out to games, out to dinner, to see special shows.

"I'd keep doing it faithfully. I'd set it up with the organization every time. I just wouldn't want to be confined to every Thursday night. I even know which organization I'd like to do this for." It was a religious youth organization he had never been involved with before. "But, I can't just go in there and offer to do that", he reasoned. "They'd think I was crazy."

What new-reality organization would be silly enough to pass up this man? No question he will put his money where he puts his time. Yet, the odds are that organization—the one he already feels connected to—does not have a job description on the shelf that quite fits this man's desired "job." Let's hope he hooks up with a creative volunteer coordinator or senior staff person.

In the new reality, volunteer programs will be operated hand-in-hand with fund-raising programs. They will be in the same offices, or right next door. The donor/volunteer will have a contact person, a Donor Services Representative, the nonprofit equivalent of your personal shopper and customer service representative rolled into one. That person will help customize your volunteer experience and interface with the people inside the organization to be sure your kookie idea for a project will work for them.

Everyone interfacing with you, as the volunteer, will treat you as a respected member of the family with the potential to become a major donor. No wild idea will be summarily discarded for lack of a job description.

In-Kind Starter Gifts

Another way new-reality volunteers/donors present themselves to organizations is as donors of in-kind goods. These are tangible items as opposed to cash. Similar to those who volunteer their time, in-kind donors are testing the waters to see how they will be treated. It allows them to stay in the driver's seat as they are checking you out.

Make it easier for them by developing Wish Lists. Wish Lists are essential in the new reality. They tell the donors what you need. They should include everything from used curtains to computer laboratories, from pots and pans to endowed scholarships. Make sure these are things you really do need. Include no price tags. Circulate the Wish Lists everywhere. Post them on your Web site. Print them in your newsletter. Enclose them in your holiday mailing. People who are interested in your organization will read them.

Make it easy for in-kind donors to give. Offer to pick up those computers or books. Invite them out to see the sad state of your current computers. Like my retired friend looking to hook up with a youth program, if someone were to happen to show him a Wish List, he would surely be forthcoming. "Oh," he might say, "New sports gear? I could do that. Oh, used, high-quality women's business suits? My wife could do that."

With each in-kind contribution, he is making more of a connection with you. He is watching to see what happens after you get the sports gear. What kind of thank you does he get? His Donor Services Representative would know kids and sports were his hot buttons and, for sure, she would invite him out to see some of the equipment put to use. She would know to treat it as one more piece of bonding in the lifelong relationship.

That sports equipment will wear out. Perhaps he would like to fund it again next year. Maybe he has a buddy in the sports equipment business. His Donor Services Representative would know that, for him, this one in-kind donation means much more than it might appear to mean. He is carving out his own customized path into the inner sanctum of the organization.

In the old reality, we were on a fishing expedition for just the size and shape of volunteers we needed. When it came to volunteer programs, the organization called the shots. In the new reality, the volunteer/donor is the boss. Our job is to listen and keep listening to hear their preferences. Out job is to engage them in the creative process of tailoring a project to their interests. We know they are building a relationship with us. We know they are a wonderful investment.

Customization Takes Time

By now, you may be thinking you can't afford this new reality approach to individual donors/volunteers. You may be concerned it will require more time and one-on-one attention than your current part-time volunteer coordinator can provide.

Consider this. I once worked as the sole development person in a super fast-paced start up program that desperately needed to raise money. I did this 15 hours a day, six or seven days a week for a couple of years. We were creating and building a new-reality, fund-raising program for an exceptional organization. Each time I had to drop everything to take that long, slow call from a volunteer with a good idea, I would kick myself. I knew it meant I would be adding precisely that much extra time to the end of my day.

One day, one of those volunteers with a crazy idea asked if he could come observe the development office in action. He thought he had an idea about how to make our fund-raising effort more efficient. "Sure," I thought cynically, "this is just what I need—to be living under the microscope of some business guy who's sure my office could be run more like a business."

He wouldn't take no for an answer. He hung around for nearly a week. At the end of the week, he presented me his "findings." "You are incredibly efficient," he said. "Between talking on the phone and inputting every detail into the computer, it's a wonder you do all you do. In fact, I can see that the only thing limiting you is hours in the day. If there were more people like you here doing more of the same, we'd be raising many times more money."

"What a surprise," I thought. "A no-brainer." Little did I know what this unique volunteer had in mind. He and I both knew I would be leaving that organization after we had set up our fund-raising system. He could see the huge head of steam we were building up in the form of happy donors. As I was leaving, he went to the board and offered to personally fund three additional positions in the development office, each for three years.

Talk about designing your own way of participating! Now, how would you categorize that wonderful man—as a volunteer, a donor, an advocate? In the new reality, these lines will completely blur. Call them friends, advocates, board members, call them what you will. Just know that they will be defining the game. If you are lucky enough to capture their attention and can comfortably follow their interests, staying closely at their side, these "volunteers" will become lifelong supporters.

CHAPTER 6

ASKING NATURALLY

Think of the last time a friend or colleague "hit you up" for a donation. You may have experienced that sinking feeling that you had "been had." You knew very little about the organization, yet because of your relationship with the person who asked you, you could not say no. You had to give. Of course, you knew the same friend or colleague would be there to reciprocate when you asked him to support your favorite charitable organization.

In the old reality, that was individual giving at its best. I call it the strong-arm-thy-Rolodex approach. And back then, in the old reality, it was the right way to raise money. The board members we cherished as "good fund-raisers" were those who could use their clout and the network of people listed in their Rolodex to raise money.

But as soon as my friend went off the board of the organization he was asking me to support and stopped "hitting me up" every year, I stopped giving there. Did that reflect badly on the organization? No. They were undoubtedly doing wonderful work. Yet, because they never took the time to win me over directly, because they never gave me the opportunity to fall in love with them directly, I stopped giving to them as soon as I felt I could.

Instead of becoming a lifelong donor for the right reasons, I was a short-term donor who left feeling resentful. Even if someone within the organization had thought to invite me out to see the place or tell me their story directly, they certainly would have put that thought aside. They would have known it was Bill who, as a board member, had been assigned to ask me for my gift. They certainly would not have wanted to interfere in any way.

In the old reality, that was the way it was done. No one gave it a second thought. People even bragged about how much they raised. Prizes, plaques, and certificates flowed freely. Annual reports abounded. No one would have thought to even question it.

In the new reality, by the time you are ready to ask a donor for a gift, the donor is ready to be asked. You have established a relationship, you have told your story to the donor. They have heard the facts about your program, listened to the first-hand testimonials, gotten teary-eyed a time or two. You have asked them enough open-ended questions to help you understand what grabs them about your program. Perhaps they have even invited some of their friends to check you out, given some of their time to work on a project, donated some used clothing or computers. They are beginning to wonder when you are going to ask them to give. That is the new reality scenario.

In the new reality, rather than strong-arming-thy-Rolodex, Asking is nothing more than "nudging the inevitable." Donors are ready to give. If you even have the thought that they are not ready to be asked, you should wait. Why would you jeopardize a lifelong relationship for one presumptuous, untimely blunder? Better to wait and cultivate, involve, and customize some more, until you are sure they're ready.

In the old reality, we were wrestling unripened fruit off the vine. In the new reality, we are picking the ripe, low-hanging fruit. Methods like strong-arming the Rolodex are now known as "interruption marketing" because they are just that—an interruption in people's lives. By today's standards, it is very "noisy" and annoying.

New reality fund raising resonates with what technology marketing guru Seth Godin calls "permission marketing." In this reality, we would never dream of insinuating donors' credit cards right out of their wallets. We know enough about the lifelong value of a donor that we would never be so foolish as to jeopardize that relationship. We would, at every turn, ask the donor's permission to proceed to the next level of courtship, letting the donor at all times be the person who drives the pace and timing of the conversation. We would know that our ultimate objective with our donors would be to earn enough trust and commitment to be worthy of their "intravenous permission" to ask them for whatever we truly need.

Once you stop worrying about the limited number of dollars out there and hoping and praying you will get your fair share, you start to relax about the whole process and treat donors as real people—the same way you would want to be treated.

Think of your favorite nonprofit. The one you'd leave your money to if you could. What is it that has you feel connected to them? Did they take wonderful care of your mother when she was ill? Does their art move you to tears? Did they teach your "learning disabled" child to read? Perhaps it wasn't something quite that personal, but somehow their mission resonates with a value you hold dear. Whether they know you personally or not, you have been following their progress, cheering them on from the sidelines.

What more could they do to involve you? To let you know they value you? To let you know what a huge difference it would make if you would give them that big gift? It probably wouldn't take much. You are already predisposed to giving to them, for whatever reason. If they were smart, once they had you on their radar screen, they would start interacting with you as a trusted, lifelong friend. They would ask for your input. They would listen to your responses. They would begin to treat you as if you were already part of the family. They would know that you are on their side. They would know their cherished issue is your cherished issue. In fact, the more they honored your natural commitment to their work—the more they opened up and shared their world with you—the more you would want to support them.

In the old reality, if we went so far as to recognize our donors by name, we still kept them at arms' length. We didn't want them snooping around. We were doing just fine without their input. In the new reality, we can't do it without them. We realize the fulfillment of our mission really does require that ongoing, rich fertilization that happens only in true dialog.

Instead of looking at the world strictly from our organization's point of view, suddenly the donors have become three-dimensional human beings with needs and concerns of their own, needs and concerns we can begin to anticipate and want to know more about.

If you treat your donors as lifelong family, for better or worse, they will stay with you forever. Once you have taken the time to get to know a donor and to recognize their genuine commitment to your work, it would be insulting to treat them any other way.

That is the new reality—donors giving because they want to give. No one is making them do it. They are giving freely. They are feeling great about it. Furthermore, they are so satisfied with their involvement with you that they are telling others about you. They are actually out there speaking your cause. You see, it is not just your work you are doing, it is their work too.

Unrestricted Annual Gifts versus Multiple-Year Pledges

In the old reality of scarce resources, gifts for unrestricted operating support were solicited one year at a time. We were thankful for whatever we got because it insured our one-year-at-a-time, hand-to-mouth existence. Only in capital campaigns might we ask people to make multiple-year pledges. We would never have wanted an annual supporter to be locked in to a multiple-year pledge for an unrestricted operating gift. After all, how could we insure they would pay up? What if we wanted to ask them again for a bigger gift before their pledge expired?

In the new reality, once we have educated our donors—one donor at a time—and let them genuinely fall in love with our work, we will know them much better. We will have asked them questions, determined their unique preferences. By the time they're ready to give it will be merely nudging the inevitable or picking the ripe, low-hanging fruit.

At that point, it would be almost insulting not to invite them into the family on a longer-term basis. Of course, they can still do the one-year-at-a-time thing. But many donors already know they want to stick around for longer. To them, a three, five, or ten year commitment to a Multiple-Year Giving Society is much more satisfying than a one-time gift. It lets them raise their hands, figuratively, and say, "Count me in." It lets them go public with their commitment to your organization. It lets them self-select into a special group that receives special treatment and special benefits. It lets them introduce others to your organization. It lets them become your advocates, spreading the word. It casts your net wider.

Nor does it in any way preclude your coming back to them within the first year and asking them to consider increasing their giving to the next level. You would never do that unannounced. It would never come as a surprise to them, because your ongoing contacts with them would be giving you the feedback about what they are ready for next, and when. You would be so tuned in to them that you could read the cues. If you had even a thought that it would be too soon to ask for more, you would wait.

You see, your multiple-year society members are in a class of their own. Their multiple-year financial pledge tells you they plan to stick around. Their multiple-year gift gives you permission to come back and ask them for more. They are telling you they are real believers in your work; that they want to be part of your family. They are letting you know that you can have more direct conversations with them about the issues that are really on your mind. These are the people you want to be going to lunch with. You will come to seek out their advice and their input. It will not be merely a token gesture on your part. It will become a true dialog. This is what will lead to happy, lifelong donors. And it is within reach of your organization.

I once worked on a project where we built a multiple-year society quickly. The entry level was $1,000 a year for five years. The next level up was $25,000 a year for five years. The third level was $20,000 (over five years) toward an endowment fund. The donors had been well enough informed, interviewed, and cultivated so they were happy to say yes.

The second year into their pledges, it became clear that this young organization was going to need a capital campaign. Rather than rush to the foundations and corporations with our hands out, we went right back to those Multiple-Year Donors and told them the straight story: a new building was needed. We invited them to see the old building if they had not already seen it, and shared with them our vision for the new building. We showed them the architects' drawings, the budget, the whole works.

We raised all the capital we needed from the first 18 Multiple-Year Donors we called on. In their minds, we were already high on their priority list. They had fallen in love with our organization for the right reasons. Their multiple-year gifts of $1,000 or $25,000, which seemed huge to us, were the tip of the iceberg to them. They were delighted to make a capital gift the second year in addition to keeping their annual operating fund pledge going.

In fact, our "fulfillment rate" on our five-year pledges—the percentage paid off— was over 95%. That did not surprise us at all. True to the principles of the new reality, we had stayed in a customized, donor-driven dialog with each of them. What did surprise us, however, was the number of Multiple-Year Donors who pre-paid their entire pledge the second year and then, wonder of wonders, signed on to do it again for another five years, often at a higher level!

In the new reality, multiple-year giving for unrestricted operating support will prevail.

CHAPTER 7

WELCOME TO THE FUTURE: GIVING ONLINE

In the old reality, if you wanted to talk to a friend or colleague, you had three modes of connecting available to you—you could send them a letter, call them on the telephone, or speak with them in person. An organization sophisticated enough to have an individual giving program used these same three media to connect to donors and potential donors.

When it came to raising funds, our first choice was usually the mail. In our fear and trepidation of having to interact with real donors, and in keeping with the mass-marketing mentality of the old reality, the mail was the medium of least resistance.

First, we calculated how much the mailing would have to yield to be worth the cost. Then, we decided whether to manage the process in-house or to out-source the entire direct-mail program to a professional firm. Then someone bought lists of the "right" names in the "right" zip codes, wrote compelling letters, mailed them in the statistically approved type of envelope with the right color of ink and type style. Then we sat back and waited for the checks to pour in.

Mail made it easy. It was highly impersonal. We never had to ask those scary donors for anything in person. After all, we had all that good demographic research to tell us what they all would want. Nothing had to be too personalized. It worked perfectly in the old reality.

If we were a bit more courageous, we upped the ante to the telephone. We could field our own team of telephone callers from our volunteers, alumni, or board to conduct our own in-house phone solicitation. Or, to keep it impersonal and lessen the in-house workload, we could contract out the phone solicitation to a sophisticated telemarketing firm that used paid "professional" callers. They were experts in the mass marketing game. They could make it yield for us.

A third approach was having people who were closely associated with our organization ask real individuals for monetary gifts in person. Though this clearly yielded the greatest return for the cost, it was not exactly everyone's favorite. The mere thought of an in-person solicitation brought out the "I hate fund raising" in most of us. Yet, as referenced in the strong-arm-thy-Rolodex section, it produced. It gave us direct contact with the ultimate decision-maker and, in most cases, immediate results.

The New Reality

While the new reality does not do away with any of these ways of raising funds, it calls for a whole new, customized approach to their use, and adds the new trump-card medium of our information age world: online giving.

While many nonprofit organizations would prefer otherwise, online giving is here to stay. It is not going away. Rather than thinking of online giving as an annoying intruder into our well-established modes of doing business, embrace it as your new best friend. Just as the online version of everything else is becoming standard fare, so too will online giving.

This is precisely because it is so ideally suited to the new reality; it defines the new reality. Online giving will become a hallmark, an icon if you will, of giving in the new reality. In fact, it will become the preferred medium for most donors. Online giving, by its very nature, affords precisely the customized, personalized dialog so essential in the new reality. Although even in the new reality nothing will ever substitute for a face-to-face, in-person relationship, the driving medium of that relationship will be the Internet. If fully embraced and woven into every aspect of your fund-raising programs, it will become your preferred medium as well.

That is not to say it will be the only medium. But the online medium provides the three essential ingredients of thriving in today's "blur" of activity: speed, connectivity and the unique blend of intangibles that each of us as individuals needs to inspire us to make a charitable gift. Why? Because the online relationship is so much faster. It can be so readily personalized. It is so much more convenient. It can be tracked and managed so much more effectively. It lets the donor determine the timing. It doesn't require a tuxedo or even a checkbook.

Imagine having thousands of loyal, ongoing donors who know and love you who prefer to talk to you and give to you online. These are donors who voluntarily, at their self-determined pace, go through the entire process of dating, courting, getting married, and growing old together with you online.

I have already seen donors who have a standing order with their investment company to direct deposit anything over a set percentage of monthly interest in their account to the charity of their choice. This past holiday season, on several occasions, I had friends and colleagues tell me they had spent the day giving away money online. One man was reveling in the joy his favorite homeless shelter would have in discovering the $35,000 he had just clicked their way.

As with the rest of the new reality, online giving won't come slamming over us like a tidal wave. That is because it is already here. Just look around and notice the extent to which your life is already conducted online. Just because my savvy, 70-something mother emails me many times a day from her comfy retirement community in Florida (in between her online bridge games and following her investments), doesn't mean she telephones me any less! In fact, now that she is emailing her grandchildren directly, she has more advice for me than ever! Her purse-sized system travels the globe with her, beaming back reports, photos and instant impressions. In other words, it won't happen the way you think. In much the same way that technology has blended into our worlds, it will meld right into the world of giving.

This may still seem a little far-fetched, given the lack of sophistication with the Internet amongst most nonprofit organizations. At the time of this writing, most employees of nonprofit organizations have access to state-of-the-art technology in their homes or other public access venues. They have at least a moderate comfort level with using the Internet. Yet their organizations are lagging woefully behind in the use of the technology tools so readily available in the for-profit world. When asked about online giving, most organizations in the know will tell you that they have a good Web site, and some will boast of a direct donation button for accepting "secured transactions." Others say proudly that they enjoy the benefits of "affinity marketing" by being listed with one or more online shopping, auction or other e-commerce sites. At best, these could be called online flirting, which misses the point and the power of this medium entirely.

In other words, many nonprofit organizations are still back in the glacial-paced, linear, old reality. They are assuming first they hire the Web master, then they build the Web site, then they have the site secured, then the donors come. That is the old reality, "If you build it, they will come" thinking. That thinking assumes these donors wake up each morning thinking of your organization, eager to seek you out, go to your fascinating Web site to learn more about you, and then hurry to click on the "Donate Now" box with a huge gift.

In fact, a Web site, as a stand-alone medium for giving, guarantees you nothing. Expecting to receive direct donations on the organization's Web site may even be a mistake for all but the largest organizations. More likely, in the new reality, sophisticated and cost-conscious nonprofit organizations will affiliate with one or more of the aggregated online giving sites or portals. These privately-funded, often for-profit sites are far more sophisticated and far better capitalized to "drive traffic" to your organization's emotionally-engaging Web site. They are in the business of playing the Internet game. They must keep up with its latest developments in order to survive. Your organization is not in the Internet business. You are in business to provide the services stated in your mission.

The new reality will be the end of the costly no-win game of trying to keep up internally with the latest information technology. Michael Gilbert, nationally known expert in the field of nonprofit organizations and technology recently said: "Nonprofit organizations can soon expect to have access to low-cost, easy-to-use applications and services which will allow them to redirect a great percentage of their resources back to their core missions. These will include knowledge-management and communication tools such as customized intranets, searchable group email systems, donor and contact management systems, cross media document publication, event and conference management and accounting and human resource processing. These applications, many of which will be invaluable to fund raising, will be offered as a customized suite of services available on a subscription basis, and accessed via inexpensive hardware and basic browser software."

For fund raising in particular, the mistake will be to back away from the power of the Internet and consider it merely an additional source of acquiring new donors. Without taking advantage of the high-touch capabilities of the online connection, customizing every single interaction based on every morsel of personal data you have earned from that donor, even the best online giving programs will become nothing more than a spiffed-up direct mail acquisition program. Without quickly making the transition to a customized dialog in order to determine what interests that specific donor in your organization, you will have missed the magic of this medium.

You will recall we said earlier that a mass-marketing donor acquisition strategy alone is a vestige of the old reality. It is no longer effective for adding new, Baby Boomer donors who are already loyal to several organizations. This is not the case, however, with newer, younger, technology-oriented donors. For many of them, charitable giving is a new experience. Clearly, their preferred medium is online. People in the Internet world will tell you that donors prefer to receive ongoing communication in the same medium in which they initially communicated with you. In other words, for some—but not necessarily all—donors, the Internet is also an ideal medium for developing a lifelong relationship.

The challenge to our organizations will be to ascertain each donor's unique preferences. Rather than being obsessed with merely acquiring these new donors, you will need to engage them in sufficient donor-directed, ongoing, personalized, meaningful dialog online to deepen your relationship. This includes being ever-alert to the virtual cues as to when they are ready to "get live". Via one medium or another, the task is still the same: getting more and more intimate with your donors. The Internet facilitates that process seamlessly.

Once they find you online, potential donors must be able to learn more about you at their own pace. They can ask you questions online, and you can respond. By providing them with the additional information they requested, you have gained their tacit permission to ask them a little more about themselves. The anonymity of the Internet lets the donor comfortably determine the pace. It keeps the entire "dating" process donor-centered.

I know of one group where a major donor, still anonymous to them, has an entire virtual relationship. He has given over $100,000 online. He requested that his most recent gift be used as a challenge to be matched by other donors. Many donors will use an online gift as a test gift to see if you even notice them.

The faster and more personal your organization's response, the better.

The second part of this book presents and develops a model for building a self-sustaining individual giving program. This entire model can be carried out online.

For example, I once worked with a national, professional organization of engineers, scientists and mathematicians for whom a total online strategy worked beautifully. We stumbled across it by a process of elimination after failing miserably in all other media. Once we realized these brainy folks preferred to communicate via their computer screens, everything fell into place.

Using strictly the online medium, we were able to meet them, tell the powerful story of the organization, get to know them, court them, and ask for multiple-year pledges for unrestricted operating support. We even conducted a virtual event to celebrate our success!

The world of online giving is here to stay. Add it to your arsenal and be willing to let it become the driving medium of your individual giving program. Do not back away from its power; embrace it. It is ideally suited to your number one goal in the new reality: building lifelong donors.

The sooner you shed the skin of the old reality, the sooner you will feel at home here. Welcome to the new reality, where donors *want* to give.

CHAPTER 8

THE RAISING MORE MONEY MODEL

This chapter will lay out a four-step model for building a self-sustaining, individual giving program. Subsequent chapters will take you step-by-step through the model in more detail. Using this model will generate lifelong donors for your organization, and it will produce the breakthrough you are committed to having.

The model is designed as a circle. Imagine a cycle, a loop, a closed circuit, an old-fashioned electric train set that just goes around and around. Once your potential donors get on board, they stay on board. The cycle starts over each time they give. Your job is to tailor this model to your organization and to keep expanding it to include as many people as possible, year after year.

The model has four essential steps which take you through the cycle.

Step One: The Point of Entry

This is where potential donors begin the cycle. The Point of Entry is a one-hour, introductory event which educates and inspires people about your organization. You do not ask for money at a Point of Entry. You should assume that every potential donor will attend only one Point of Entry event in their lifetime, so you had better make it memorable.

A Point of Entry must include three components:

1. The Facts about your organization at the basic level, including the vision and needs of the organization;

2. An Emotional Hook so compelling people will never forget it; and

3. A system to legitimately Capture the Names, addresses, phone numbers, and emails of the guests who attend.

Step One: The Point of Entry

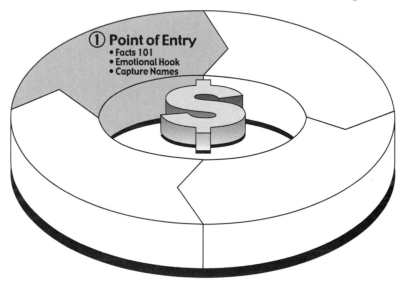

The classic Point of Entry event is a tour. Research shows that people who actually set foot in your office or facility will give more than people who have never been there. If your organization in any way lends itself to a tour, that should be the Point of Entry you use. Even if you think there is not much for people to see on your tour, there are ways to add the missing elements. If confidentiality issues are a concern, there are many ways to compensate, often using video and live or written testimonials.

If you feel a tour absolutely will not work for you, there are many other formats you can use. For example, you can have a box-lunch Point of Entry event in a board member's conference room, a reception at someone's home, or a one-on-one meeting, either formal or informal. In these cases, you will need the video, testimonials, and your compelling visionary leader to speak briefly. The venue is less relevant than being sure you have included all three essential ingredients.

Your Point of Entry must give people a sense of how the work of your organization changes lives. Even if you are dealing with an abstract policy issue, there is a way to boil it down to the impact it has on one life. As individuals, we are emotional donors looking for rational reasons to justify our emotional decision to give. In other words, your Point of Entry event must satisfy both the head and the heart.

Just imagine for a moment that you are visiting an organization for the first time.

Scenario 1: They dazzle you with the facts—the extent of the problem in society, the number of people served, the breadth and quality of services, the gap still remaining to be filled. You are impressed. "Very interesting," you say. But you are not yet impressed enough to give. The facts alone won't move you to act.

Scenario 2: No facts, they just start right in with the emotion—photos, video, testimonials about the lives that have been altered thanks to this organization. You are hooked emotionally, but it is still not enough to get you to give. You are suspicious. What are the facts? How will they actually use the money? What is their track record?

Solution: Your Point of Entry event has to intertwine facts and emotion so that, before they even realize it, the guests are satisfied. If you don't accomplish both, you won't have a foundation from which to launch a relationship with a lifelong donor.

The Facts must include:

- A brief history of the organization;
- A basic statement of the programs and services offered;
- The numbers: people served, budget size, etc.; and
- The vision for the future including a clear statement of what you will need to get there. You have to clearly identify the gap. You can easily do this while highlighting your strengths. "As wonderful as this program is, there are still 2,000 children in our area going unserved." "If only we had the computers and other equipment we need to train our people properly."

A good way to highlight your needs is with a Wish List. This is one of the essential handouts at a Point of Entry event. Be sure your Wish List has a wide assortment of needs, from band-aids to science laboratories, from old curtains to endowed chairs. Do not include price tags, just the items you and your staff need.

Finally, you must be sure you have a legitimate way to Capture the Names, addresses, phone numbers and email of every guest. After all, if the Point of Entry is just the first point in a cycle of lifelong giving, you will need to know how to contact each person again. If you have been straightforward in your invitation to the Point of Entry in the first place, this should be no problem.

We will cover the Point of Entry in more detail in the next chapter and the Emotional Hook will be covered in Chapter 10.

Step Two: Follow Up and Involve

The second step on the circle of a self-sustaining, individual giving program is making a personal Follow-Up Call within a week to each person who attended the Point of Entry event.

The Follow-Up Call is not a standard thank-you, for which a note would suffice. It is an interactive research call. Think of it as a one-on-one focus group in which you gather critical data on each potential lifelong donor and friend.

Step Two: Follow Up

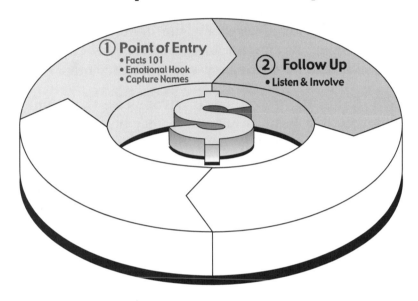

The Follow-Up Call follows a specific, five-point format which will help you get the information you need.

Point 1. Thank them for coming. You certainly need to thank them. They are busy people who did not need to take their time to come to your Point of Entry event.

Point 2. What did they think (of the tour, the organization, the issue)?

Point 3. This is the hardest step for most of us, and by far the most critical component of the Follow-Up Call: Stop talking and listen. In this model, the more you listen, the more you will notice potential donors are telling you exactly how they would like to become involved with your organization. But, if you are too busy talking or planning what you want to say next, you will miss all the rich cues.

Point 4. If they have not already told you, ask: Is there any way you could see yourself becoming involved with our organization? You let them tell you. In the new reality of donor-centered, individual giving, the donors have their own ideas—ideas that may not mesh with your needs. You still need to listen and be open to saying yes to what they offer.

Point 5. Finally, ask if there is anyone else they think you should invite to a Point of Entry. You may be surprised to discover that, because you have taken the time to listen at each step along the way, people will be so appreciative they will naturally suggest others you should contact. Even people who are honest enough to tell you your issue is not their hot button will have other people for you to invite. Ask if they would mind if you contact these people directly and use their name. Then do it.

Every bit of data you gather should be recorded in your database. Be sure your computer system has a good section for you to record notes about each contact with each donor.

You are sure to come across people who are *not* interested in getting more involved with your organization. The Follow-Up Call is where you can let them off the hook. Don't even think about taking it personally. Put yourself in their shoes. They took their time to come to the Point of Entry event. Yes, they were touched and impressed with what you do, they may even send you a little check as a courtesy. But they are deeply involved in another cause that is their true passion. While they like you and know that you are doing good work, you are never going to make it to the top third of their giving list.

Let them go graciously. Thank them sincerely for taking their time to come. If they are open enough to mention the other issue or organization they are involved with, compliment it. Honor their commitment and dedication to that cause. Do not even offer to send them an envelope they can use to make a small gift. Let them completely off the hook. It will disarm them and distinguish you from the others. Think of how grateful you would feel if people heard you the first time when you really meant, "No."

In the long run, these people will help you in many ways, primarily by referring others. Many times, people have told me, "This type of program just isn't my thing, I'm deeply involved in [another organization], and that's where I want to be putting my resources right now." Then, when I asked them the final question about whom they know who might want to come to a Point of Entry tour, they would often say, "You should definitely call my wife (or my work colleague or my friend Marcia). This is definitely the kind of thing they'd be interested in. Tell them I recommend they come out and take your tour." What better compliment than for a person to refer you to others and encourage you to use their name? In the long run, you will have made a real friend, just by letting someone off the hook.

Remember, this is a model for building lifelong donors— donors who are so interested in your mission that they want to stay with you. It's as if, one by one, you are selecting the people who are going to be part of your organization's family forever. You do not want to select someone who is not really interested. There are so many generous and caring folks who truly understand what you are doing. They are the ones you are on a scouting mission to find.

Step Three: Asking for Money

The third step in our model is to Ask for Money. Notice you have not done that at either Step One, the Point of Entry event, or at Step Two, the Follow-Up Call. You have been busy warming up and screening people to see if they would make a loyal lifelong donor. In our model, by the time you get around to Asking for Money, you should be certain that the person is ready to give.

Step Three: Asking for Money

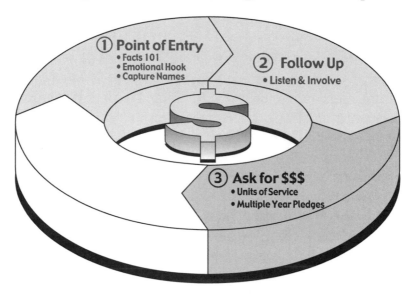

In the old reality, the "Ask" often happened right away, before the person had a chance to buy in, head and heart, to the mission of the organization. In the new reality, there is no need for that. In fact, if you have any question that the person may not be ready to give, don't ask yet. Trust your instincts and hold off until they are ready.

Asking is very much like picking the ripe, low-hanging fruit from a fruit tree. When a person first comes to your Point of Entry event, they are brand new to your organization, completely unripened fruit. By taking them through the tour, they begin to ripen and with the Follow-Up Call they ripen further. By the time you get around to asking them for money, it should be nothing more than "nudging the inevitable"—like easily picking a piece of fruit off a tree the moment it is ready. On the other hand, if you wait too long, what happens? The fruit becomes overripe, falls to the ground and spoils. In other words, in the life cycle of each donor, there are perfect moments for asking for money. You have to tune your radar to those moments.

The Cultivation Superhighway

In this model, everything between Step Two, the Follow-Up Call and Step Three, the "Ask", is called the Cultivation Superhighway, which is discussed in detail in Chapter 13. The more contacts you have with a potential donor along the superhighway, the more money they will give you when you ask. There is a direct correlation between the number of contacts and the size of the gifts received.

The Cultivation Superhighway

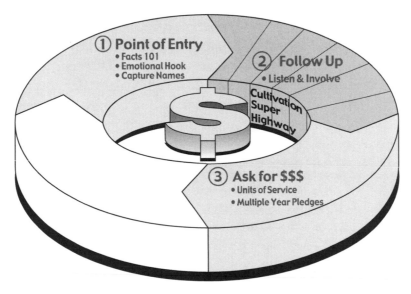

This should come as no surprise. Again, think of yourself as that donor. Imagine that an organization had already taken the time to educate you and follow up personally. The more you heard from a real person at that organization directly and the more specifically their calls, emails, faxes, or meetings with you related to your specific needs, the more inclined you would be to give a larger gift the next time they asked.

It is worth considering what qualifies as a contact. Is it mailing a potential donor your newsletter or invitations to upcoming events? Yes, those count as contacts, but nothing substitutes for a person-to-person, live contact. The best of these contacts are dictated by the donor. If they are generous enough in the Follow-Up Call to tell you how they might like to become more involved, your job is to stay in contact with them to make those things happen. Keep following up; keep giving them feedback.

If for example, they would like to help you start a new program you would love to have, you will need to invite them back to meet with the key staff in that area, with the board, or with the director. Or there may be other folks from the community that the potential donor would also like to involve. Having them invite others to find out about your organization at a Point of Entry event is also a key indicator of their support.

If you have done your homework and tended to their needs and interests throughout all your contacts with them, this person will become a self-proclaimed volunteer for your organization. While their project may not fit into your normal job description for a volunteer, in the new reality of raising funds from individuals, this person is a volunteer with a customized, self-designed job description.

Eighty-four percent of all charitable contributions come from households in which one or more family members volunteer. In other words, being a volunteer is a key indicator of giving. While the research doesn't specify that volunteers give to the same organizations where they volunteer their time, it does show that giving follows involvement. And in the new reality of individual giving, you should assume that giving will follow involvement, even loosely defined involvement.

Donors need to know that you need them and that their contribution will make a difference in accomplishing your mission. They need to know that you are responsive to their suggestions. In many cases, they need to know that you need them for more than their money. So, the more meaningful the contacts, the better. Contacts are what ripens the fruit.

Asking

When the timing is right for asking, the first thing to consider is the medium you will use. Will you ask in person, over the telephone, online, at an event, or by mail? Any of these is acceptable although, generally speaking, the bigger the gift you are after, the more face-to-face and one-to-one the Ask needs to be.

If you have brought many people through your Points of Entry in a short span of time, then followed up and involved them to their satisfaction, you may well find yourself in the enviable position of having many people to ask for a contribution at about the same time. In that case, the Free One-Hour Asking Event is ideal. (See Chapter 22.) The critical mass of true believers in the same room will produce breakthrough results in an hour.

On the other hand, if people have been trickling through your Point of Entry events more slowly, or if you are starting with Points of Re-Entry for prior donors, you may do better making your Asks one-on-one, in person or by phone. If your donors prefer online communication, this entire model can be done online. For those donors, an online Ask may be preferable.

Regardless of the medium or venue for your Ask, in this model every Ask must include two essential ingredients.

Units of Service

First, you must ask for specific amounts. We call them Units of Service. They are the giving levels, gift clubs—gimmicks, if you will. They are the bite-sized chunks of unrestricted funding that one person can support.

You do not need more than three Units of Service, and there should be a significant gap in their dollar levels. In the new reality, the lowest level will be $1,000 or $83 a month. Many people who truly love you and want to be lifelong members of your family can and will give at that level. In fact, many may already be giving at that level when you total up their many gifts each year.

We will talk later about how to design your Units of Service. For now, the key thing to know is that these levels are gimmicks, and in the new reality of lifelong donors it is fine to tell people that. If they are brought into your mission fully, they will trust you to use the money for the overall programs of the organization. They know that someone has to pay the light bill and the salaries. They know they can look at your annual audit if they want to see exactly how the money was spent.

Multiple-Year Pledges

The second essential ingredient in Asking for Money is that you ask people to become a part of your Multiple-Year Society by making a multiple-year pledge for Units of Service. That's right, you ask them to commit at the time of their first pledge to give that same amount each year for a specified number of years. Why? Not for the reason you may think. As wonderful as

Asking For Money:
Two Essential Ingredients

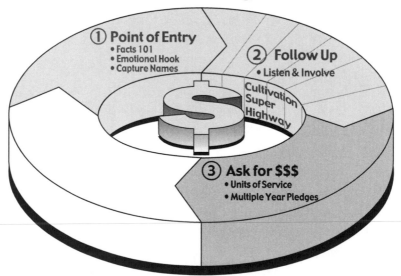

it is for your organization to know you have the stability of all those pledges waiting to be collected each year, that is not the main reason for asking for multiple-year pledges.

The reason is for the donor. It allows donors to declare themselves as part of your organization's family. It gives a particular group of more committed donors the opportunity to say: "You can count on me. I'm a long-term believer in what you are up to."

Think for a moment about your own giving, that mental list you made earlier of all the places you've been supporting over the years, getting relatively little feedback in return. What if someone from that organization was to call you and say: "Hello, Ms. Jones, we notice you have been a loyal donor for the last 15 years. Thank you for your support. We are calling to ask if you would be willing to make a pledge to give that *same* level of gift for the next five years." You would have a hard time saying no, right? After all, the odds are you will keep giving there indefinitely.

The value of the Multiple-Year Society is that it allows donors to "go public" with their commitment and support. Most of us are very private in our giving. We just keep sending in our little, or not so little, check year after year. We aren't looking for any recognition. We each have our personal reasons for giving. We don't even talk about our giving with others. The satisfaction of giving is often more than enough.

By making a multiple-year pledge, we know that our name will be listed in the Multiple-Year Society. Others may notice. Moreover, it gives us license to talk about our fondness for this organization with those close to us—family and friends, the people we trust, respect, and confide in. Our natural tendency as a person who has made that multiple-year commitment is to share our enthusiasm with others.

Step Four: Multiple-Year Donors Introducing Others

This leads to the fourth step in our model where individual donors who have joined the Multiple-Year Society introduce

Step Four: Donors Introduce Others

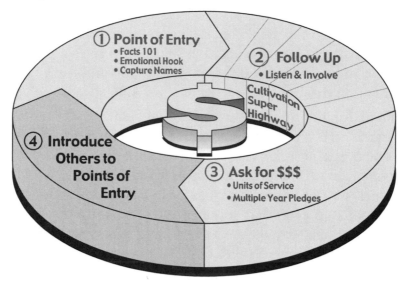

others to the organization. How? By inviting them to a Point of Entry. They know, since they have been through the cycle with us, that we will take good care of their friends. We will educate and inspire them at a Point of Entry, Follow Up personally, involve them as appropriate or let them off the hook graciously if they are not interested. They trust the organization to treat their friends with respect. Their secret hope, of course, is that their friends will fall in love with the organization too—in their own right, for their own reasons—and become lifelong donors as well.

That completes the first circuit around the model for a brand-new donor.

This Cycle Spirals Upward

The breakthrough your organization is after calls for lifelong donors. To keep your donors in the cycle, every Multiple-Year Society donor is invited to two or three Free Feel-Good Cultivation Events during the year. (These are also called Points of

Re-Entry.) As the name implies, these events serve to reconnect them to the facts and emotion of your work.

These Free Feel-Good Cultivation Events can be regularly scheduled events having to do with the work of the organization, such as a graduation of your program's participants or a lecture on a topic of interest. Or they can be events planned specially for these donors. You may even choose to have different events for donors at different levels. In any case, these events reinforce the wise investment the donors have made in your organization.

Following each Free Feel-Good Cultivation Event or Point of Re-Entry, every donor receives another one-on-one Follow-Up Call, asking a few more open-ended questions selected from the Treasure Map Interview questions in Chapter 11, including asking them to suggest others to be invited to a Point of Entry event. This in turn leads to more cultivation, more involvement, deeper and deeper permission or trust. Whatever they tell you in each Follow-Up Call determines the frequency and quality of involvement they would like to have, including the timing of the next Ask.

After the next gift is received, another Follow-Up Call is made to say thank you, there is more conversation, and on it goes. All the while you are looking and listening for how else they might want to become involved, inviting them to take on a leadership role, key volunteer, or board position, as appropriate.

Ideally, in the course of the year, you have three or four occasions for personal, one-on-one contact with each donor. This contact can be made by your lead development staff person or other key staff or by one of your volunteer Donor Service Representatives (akin to a customer service representative in a bank) who is assigned to that donor for two years at a time. These contacts are nothing intrusive or artificial, but rather a natural give and take, either triggered by gifts received or their participation in one of your Free Feel-Good Cultivation events.

Can you see the exponential effect as this simple circle becomes a spiral, with an ever-growing number of Multiple-Year Donors? Now that you have seen an outline of the model, we will go deeper into each component and how you can tailor it to your organization.

CHAPTER 9

STEP ONE:
THE POINT OF ENTRY

Let's go back through the model one step at a time, beginning with the Point of Entry.

Remember, the Point of Entry is the starting point in building your organization's self-sustaining cycle of individual giving. It is a one-hour, sizzling yet succinct introduction to your organization at the basic level.

It must contain enough facts and emotion to make a lasting impact on each and every guest. No one is asked to give money at a Point of Entry event. Because you should assume each donor will attend only one full-fledged Point of Entry event in their lifetime, do your best to make it memorable!

You are aiming to design a generic Point of Entry program, one you can repeat easily and often. There are three essential ingredients every Point of Entry must include:

- The Facts about your organization
- The Emotional Hook
- Capture the Names of each visitor

Without all three of these ingredients, you might have a nice event or gathering, but it will not be a Point of Entry.

Most often, the Point of Entry will be an event, a gathering of real people in real time, to learn about your program. The classic Point of Entry event is a tour. If your organization lends itself at all to a tour, this should definitely be your preferred Point of Entry.

Even if you think there would not be much for people to see at your office, there is a lot you can do to spice it up and turn it into the perfect venue for a Point of Entry event. You can add photos to the walls and tell a story about what goes on in each room as you walk people through. Stopping by the desk of a hard-working staff person to have them share an anecdote about a child or adult who has benefitted from their program will make a big impact, as will showing an outstanding video or having someone read a testimonial in your conference room.

If you are concerned about the confidential nature of what people might see on a tour, there are ways to highlight only the programs or clients you want them to see. Many excellent Points of Entry have been done in one room only, without ever walking people through the facility. If you paint a powerful picture, people will remember it. But there is no question that people will feel much more connected to your organization, and will remember you best, if they have physically been to your site.

If you conclude you cannot have an on-site tour, here are some other examples of venues for Points of Entry:

- A box lunch at a board member's office
- Evening "house parties" in people's homes
- A one-on-one meeting anywhere
- An alumni gathering in each of your regions or cities
- An online Point of Entry event
- A self-contained Point of Entry mailer that includes a video, a written testimonial letter, and a list of questions for discussion

Note that your Point of Entry does not need to be done in a group. Once you are comfortable with the key elements of the format, you should be able to take it anywhere. You could do a one-on-one Point of Entry with a person sitting next to you on an airplane or standing next to you in a long line. It doesn't have to take a long time.

You may also discover that you have existing events which can be retooled a bit to become Points of Entry. For example: dinner parties and smaller "cultivation" events, arts performances and rehearsal nights, house parties, alumni weekends, scheduled speaking presentations to community groups, awards dinners, anniversary events, school graduations.

As you become more comfortable with this model, you will see many special events you now call "fund raisers" could easily be converted to Point of Entry events, even if you charge a fee. Rather than someone leaving your golf tournament or dinner auction merely entertained, if you include the three essential ingredients in your program, they will have attended a Point of Entry. You will then be able to Follow Up and get them on your cycle of individual giving, if they are truly interested.

The risk in doing this, of course, is that people will not know in advance that the golf tournament or Western party includes a Point of Entry element. In other words, you did not get their permission in advance to educate and inspire them. They thought they were just coming to have a good time. At a tour or single-purpose Point of Entry event, you can be more straightforward. And the more above-board you can be with your donors right from the start, the more they will trust you.

Whatever the venue, your Point of Entry events must be easy for you to conduct on a repeat basis. The more often you change locations or hosts or time of day, the more you complicate things for yourself. Keep it simple. At the school where this model was developed, once we got our Point of Entry event format refined, we were conducting breakfast tours as often as three times a week. I could arrive at the school, take out my Point of Entry box, complete with name tags, sign in sheets, handouts, pens, brochures, and other supplies and set up the event in half an hour.

Program Format

Let's walk though each element of your one-hour program.

Greeting: From the perspective of the guests, the Point of Entry event begins as they arrive and are greeted at the door or even at the curb. In Seattle, for our rainy morning Point of Entry events at a somewhat hard-to-find location, I would often stand out at the curb under an umbrella to greet people as they drove up. Be prepared to do whatever it takes to make your guests feel comfortable as they arrive.

Think about who will greet each of your visitors and where they will be stationed. Ideally, the greeter will be the person who invited them—friend, board member, etc. The next best choice is the development director or the person who will be their ongoing liaison with the organization. Note that you may want to save the executive director or chief executive officer for cameo roles later.

The greeter welcomes the guests, takes their coats and walks with them to the sign-in table.

Sign-In: This is an essential checkpoint through which all visitors must pass. A friendly, detail-oriented staff person or volunteer, seated behind the table, gives them a sign-in card and waits while they fill it out. The only information you have enough permission to gather at this early stage is their name, address, phone number (whichever one they want to give you), email address, and the name of the person who invited them to the Point of Entry event.

If you have enough guests to warrant it, name tags should be provided at the sign-in table as well.

Brief Mix and Mingle Time: As the rest of the guest are gathering, offer each guest a cup of coffee or tea, if appropriate, and introduce them to other visitors. This is a good time for the executive director to enter and be available for informal conversations. Point out pictures on the walls or any key features of the room they are in.

The Program: Everyone is seated. This is critical. Do not ever attempt to have a Point of Entry event if people are standing up (unless, of course, they are walking around on a tour). If you want them to focus, give them a seat. At their place, waiting for them, is a packet of handouts.

The program begins with a welcome greeting from the board member or volunteer who is hosting the Point of Entry event or, in their absence, the most senior fund development staff member present. This person should take a moment to tell how they became involved with the organization.

You should allow 15-20 minutes maximum for the program. You will probably want to have two speakers, the executive director, founder, or visionary leader and the development director or designated fund-raising person who will be making the Follow-Up Call. You want to be sure the follow-up person is prominently placed in the program so people will remember him or her.

Here are all of the elements that must be covered in this section.

The Facts

1. A brief history of the organization—when was it founded, by whom, how has it evolved and grown since then?

2. The mission and underlying philosophy. Why does the organization really exist?

3. A quick overview of your programs and services, at the most basic level. Resist the temptation to elaborate. Guests who want more information on a particular program can stay and talk with you at the end. Given that you are beginning a lifelong relationship, you will have plenty of time to gradually provide the specific information they need timed to their curiosity and interest.

4. The numbers. Number of people served, size of budget, sources of funding, pie charts, etc. The easiest way to cover this is to walk them quickly through the Fact Sheet in their packet.

5. The vision for the future, including the gap that will need to be filled if you are to fulfill your mission. You may want to quantify in dollars what it will cost to meet those needs. Donors today must see a clear gap and know that you have a vision for filling it. They must see where they can be useful. They are looking for how their participation can make a difference.

Questions and Answers: At the end of this informational segment of the Point of Entry event, the executive director and staff ask for questions from the guests. Allow time for three or four questions. Invite those with more questions to stay after the meeting to talk further.

The Emotional Hook

The second essential ingredient at a Point of Entry is the Emotional Hook. Remember that as individuals, we are first and foremost, emotional donors. Then we justify our emotional decision to give with the Facts. Assuming this will be the one and only Point of Entry for each guest, your Emotional Hook has got to move them.

The *true* Emotional Hook for your organization, as we will see in Chapter 10, is a complex mix of the emotions, values, stereotypes and dreams your work stirs up in people. This "internal" Emotional Hook may not be something you ever say out loud. It is the deeper story and compelling, instinctive feeling that moves people to jump in and take action. At your Point of Entry event, you definitely want to stir up this internal Emotional Hook while at the same time demonstrating the more obvious, "external" Emotional Hooks such as the cute kids or the hard-working families, either by meeting these people firsthand or through testimonials, a video, or stories.

In the old fund-raising reality, our foremost concern was protecting the privacy and dignity of our clients, families, children, artists, etc. We were so focused on not wanting to exploit anyone's situation that we went overboard in the other direction. We consciously avoided eliciting any emotion about our work. We wanted to be very professional. Fund raising became almost clinical. Is it any wonder we now find ourselves in the world of golf tournaments and other events designed to deflect attention from the real mission of the organization?

In the new fund-raising reality, this seems ridiculous. If we assume people naturally want to get involved in our work, why would we withhold the core of it? Wouldn't we want them to know the facts about child abuse? Wouldn't we want them to hear a first-hand testimonial from a former client, family member, or staff member? Wouldn't we want them to hear directly from a rural villager about the impact of that environmental issue on his family?

The Emotional Hook answers the question: How does the work of this organization impact the life of one individual? How does it affect real people? Whether your mission is related to saving whales or saving orphans, the fund-raising dollars you are looking for are going to come from real people—people with a pre-programmed frame of reference: themselves. Without even realizing it, they will be asking themselves: How does this really work? How much of an impact does this really have on one ordinary person like me? How important is it to me that this problem be solved?

Do not be afraid to use emotion. Today's donors are hungry for it. They are counting on you to inspire them. In fact, many would say that in our "high-tech" world, "high-touch" is more valued than ever. Your organization offers your donors high touch. Don't hold back on using it. And keep it simple. Your goal is to provide and experience and paint a picture in people's minds— an indelible picture. It needs to move them to tears.

The easiest way to provide an Emotional Hook for guests at your Point of Entry is through stories. Use any or all of the following elements to tell your story. Keep it brief and to the point.

Tour: Let people see your compelling work firsthand. Intersperse each stop on the tour with anecdotes. You are painting a picture as you walk people through the building. Keep high-lighting the needs.

Video: Before you consider producing a new video, consider what you may already have. A brief news clip about your orga-nization, wrapped with verbal remarks to put it in context and add the missing points, can be excellent. If you are part of a national organization, check to see what generic video material is available to you. You might even excerpt a portion of the national material and combine it with your local story.

If you must make a new video, try to get it donated or get special funding to produce it. Consider hiring a producer who has worked in television news. They are experts at painting a succinct emotional picture with images, words and music that both educate and move the audience.

Testimonials: Make it easy on yourself. If you are planning to do regular Point of Entry events, you won't want to have to find a new live testimonial speaker each time. Besides which, testimonial speakers can be inconsistent in telling their stories. A video of two or three testimonials, each highlighting a differ-ent aspect of your program, can be extremely effective. You can also use an audiotape or try having a staff member read a testi-monial from a client or family member. These can often be more moving than listening to the original author of the testimonial.

Thank you and wrap up: Be sure you conclude on time. If the last segment of your Point of Entry event is the tour, end by bringing the group back to the front door. Thank them for tak-ing their time to come. Let them know you would like to call them in the next week to get their feedback and advice.

I do not recommend doing a group debriefing or group feed-back session at the end. One person's feedback or complaint may never have occurred to the others and may only serve to distract and confuse your happy guests. There will be plenty of time for debriefing your guests one-on-one.

Handouts at Your Point of Entry

Do not overwhelm people at Point of Entry events with printed materials. When they arrive, have the following three items waiting at their places at the table:

Your basic brochure: It does not need to be your slickest five-color version. The basic model will do.

The Fact Sheet: After you have had a few Point of Entry events, the questions people need answered most often will become obvious. That is the time to make up a Fact Sheet.

The Fact Sheet should be one side of one page and no more. It is not intended to be a substitute for your basic brochure. It should contain five or six key points about your services. Most likely, you will not have space to mention all of your programs. While each program seems essential to you, your guests do not need that level of detail. Figure out a way to cluster your programs and explain them simply. Have the information on the Fact Sheet follow the format you will be using at the Point of Entry event. That way you can walk your guests right through the Fact Sheet as you go.

The Fact Sheet should also be inviting to the reader. Do not cram it full of text. You may want to use a question and answer format. Allow plenty of white space. Graphics are good; for example, you could include a pie chart about your budget or programs. The beauty of a one-page homemade Fact Sheet is you can change it easily. As you tune in to the questions people ask repeatedly, you can modify it. Consider your Fact Sheet a work in progress—just like your organization.

The Wish List: The Wish List is an essential handout at a Point of Entry event. Do not overlook it. Take the time to interview your staff to develop a list of real items they would love to have. You can cluster the items by program—the preschool's wish list, the high school's wish list—or by any other subgroup—the teachers' list, the students' list, the administration's list. Make the items personal: cooking supplies for a family of four, a computer and workstation for an elementary school classroom. There should be *no price tags* on the Wish List. Just list the items, small, medium, and large.

People will glance at the Wish List during your Point of Entry event program. The Wish List lets them know where they can fit in and contribute right away. It suggests an easy, non-threatening way to test out what it would be like to be in a relationship with your organization.

Other Frequently Asked Questions about Points of Entry

Q: *Should we give our Point of Entry events a name?*

A: Yes, by all means. The term "Point of Entry" is for your internal use only. It is much too clinical to use with the general public. Come up with a clever, inviting name. A workshop participant from an organ-donor program named their Point of Entry events "Lifesaver Events." One Red Cross chapter named theirs "The Red Cross Experience." Other groups call theirs by the name of their organization followed by "101," as in "Youth Center 101".

Q: *What is the ideal time of day to have a Point of Entry event?*

A: This can take a bit of experimenting. Start by considering the convenience of the guests. Are these working folks who would prefer something before or after work? For retired people or moms with school-age kids, lunchtime may be best.

Think about their proximity to your location. While you may think you are "only 20 minutes away," that may be more than they can spare. In that case, you may want to take your Point of Entry event on the road to them at their preferred time and location.

Next, consider the best time for viewing your organization in action. If most of your programs are in the evenings or on weekends, those might work best. One Habitat for Humanity affiliate used their Saturday morning new home dedications as their Point of Entry event. A church-based retirement center held their Point of Entry events on Sunday afternoons as open houses for families and served a light lunch.

Q: *What about serving food at a Point of Entry?*

A: The less food, the better. Not only does it add an extra layer of detail and distraction (also known as "fund-raising fluff") to your workload, it also triggers certain customary obligations for repayment. You may find that people send in small contributions after a Point of Entry event, thinking this will be their one-and-only gift. I recommend sticking to muffins and coffee, or tea and cookies, maybe some light snack food.

Q: *What is the most effective way to get people to come to our Point of Entry events?*

A: For some organizations the most challenging aspect of setting up a Point of Entry event system will be figuring out how to get people to attend. By far the most effective way to get people to come is a personal invitation from someone they know. A telephone invitation seems to work best. While, in this model, we would never want people to give money based on a sense of obligation to the person who introduced them to the organization, that very same sense of obligation or repayment may be precisely what is needed to get them to come to your Point of Entry event.

Q: *What about using printed invitations?*

A: While you can certainly follow up the phone call with a postcard or fancy invitation which confirms the date, do not delude yourself into thinking that printed materials alone will ever incite even one person to attend anything. While they may be useful for informing a broader audience that you are now offering tours or open houses, a printed invitation or a letter, even if it has a personal note from their best buddy, is no longer sufficient to deliver a real person at your event. Ultimately, it will take at least one phone call, and perhaps more, to reconfirm the guests a day or two before the event.

While some people will attend strictly because they are interested in your mission or programs or because they have heard about your stellar reputation, the vast majority will come to their initial Point of Entry event primarily out of a sense of obligation to the person who invited them.

Q: *Where should we start? Who should we invite first?*

A: Start with the "easy" people, the people who already know and love your organization. It will reconnect them to their passion for your work. Once they understand how a Point of Entry event works, they will naturally want to invite others.

Another group of "easy" people are those who have a natural self-interest in your mission or programs or who have heard about your stellar reputation and are curious to know more. In fund raising, self-interest is a good thing. We will talk more about it in Chapter 11.

Q: *Do you have a suggested "script" for people to use when inviting others to Point of Entry events?*

A: Here is a script you can use as a guideline:

"As you may know, I serve on the board of _____. We are realizing that we need to do a better job of telling our story to the community. We have started to offer little one-hour tours for people to see our programs firsthand and to give us feedback on how we can get the word out to more people.

I would love to have you come out and take the tour and meet the real visionary who is our director and some of the great staff. You won't be asked for any money. The dates are _____."

Q: *How can we involve our board in the Point of Entry event process?*

A: After you have done a dry-run Point of Entry event for your staff, have your first real Point of Entry event be a "demo, kick-the-tires" Point of Entry event for your board. Tell them you would like to start a program of tours or open houses or house parties to spread the word in the community about your good work. This is strictly for informational purposes. No one will be asked to give money at the Point of Entry event. Tell them you want their input first, as the board. Schedule one in the next month, preferably at a separate time from the regularly-scheduled board meeting.

Encourage them to invite someone close to them who may never have visited your program before. Perhaps it will be someone in their family who has heard a lot about your organization but has never seen it firsthand. By having a few real guests at the "demo" Point of Entry event, it is less likely to feel like a standard board meeting. People will be on their best behavior for "company," and they will be watching the reactions of the real guests.

Make this "demo" Point of Entry event exceptional. Your goal is to have your own board members be re-inspired and reconnected to their passion for the organization. Have it be your very best shot at what your ideal Point of Entry events will look like in the future. After this demo Point of Entry event, either individually by phone or in a group at the next board meeting, take the time to debrief with the board members. Take extensive notes on all their feedback and make the changes they suggest wherever possible.

After all, you want the board members to feel safe inviting their friends in the future. If you expect the board to jump in and invite people, you have got to let them kick the tires and have input into reshaping the format and content. They have to be able to count on each subsequent Point of Entry event delivering that same generic impact of the organization's story, both facts and emotion. They must be able to trust that their friends will not be asked for money at the Point of Entry event. Paying attention to the special concerns of board members will be well worth it.

Once you begin having Point of Entry events, you must keep your board actively involved. Here are some tips for doing that.

1. At each board meeting, ask the host from the prior month's Point of Entry event to talk about it. Have them share poignant or exciting anecdotes. Be sure to have them stress how easy and convenient it was to host the event and how much their friends and the other guests enjoyed it.

2. Give each board member a list of everyone who attended a Point of Entry event the prior month along with the name of the person who invited them. Be sure those who invite their friends are sufficiently thanked.

3. Allow a little time for people to comment on the names on these lists and to "network" a bit about others they plan to invite. Often a call from a second board member will insure a guest's attendance.

4. Schedule Point of Entry events for the entire next year. Publish the dates for internal use. Give copies to the board and staff, post them on internal calendars, bulletin boards, and so on.

5. Ask each board member to consider hosting one Point of Entry event. Though you will only be counting on them to attend and do the "welcome," that Point of Entry event will be a perfect opportunity for them to invite their friends to attend as well. If their friends can't make it that day, the board member can suggest one of the other dates and offer to call the board host for that event to let them know their guest will be coming.

6. Print up business cards with the name and address of the organization on the front and the dates of the upcoming Point of Entry events and driving directions on the back. Have stacks of these cards available at each board meeting for people to carry with them throughout the month. As they are out and about, talking with their friends and associates, it will be easy for them to invite people to the events and leave them with a card.

7. Be sure to remind people to reconfirm each guest the day or night before. This tells the guests that you are really counting on them. Many guests confess it was the final reminder call that put to rest their last-minute thoughts about not showing up. If you are still not sure they will make it, you may need to offer to pick them up. Sometimes, just the anticipation of having to search out a new place can be a deterrent. You want to remove as many barriers as possible.

Q: *How do we involve our staff in the Point of Entry events?*

A: The staff are your treasure! It is in your best interest, if you are the person responsible for individual giving, to take the time to earn their support. You will gain an entirely new perspective on your organization, in the process.

When you create your Treasure Map (Chapter 11), you will notice the key role that staff play as a common link between your board members, your volunteers, your vendors, your clients, members or constituents, and other community groups. They provide a number of resources to the organization—their expertise, their commitment, their time and hard work—and they also have a strong self-interest in having your fund-raising program succeed.

At the same time, this may not always be apparent to them in the face of the front-line issues they deal with everyday. Have a little compassion for the staff to be the dedicated, program-centered people they are. Without them you wouldn't have a program to raise money for. Here are some suggestions:

1. Meet with your staff as a whole or in subgroups to explain the new Point of Entry program you will be starting in order to build lifelong donors. You may need to do a mini-training to show them the model and invite their input.

2. Put on a special Point of Entry event just for the staff and invite their critical feedback. Let them tell you how they would like you to describe their program to visitors.

3. Get them talking about what keeps them working here, doing their work day to day. Notice whether or not their stories inspire you. This may be the source of your Emotional Hook.

4. Tell them clearly and honestly how your Point of Entry events will affect them. If it includes a tour, you may be intruding on their daily work as you bring visitors through. Will you want them to speak at the Point of Entry or to share stories from the front lines?

5. You might want to show them your Treasure Map (Chapter 11), or make a new one with them, to get them thinking of additional people to invite to the Points of Entry events. This might be the perfect opportunity for them to finally invite their friends and family to come and see firsthand where they work. Remember, everyone is welcome at a Point of Entry event. You never know who is in *their* Treasure Map.

6. Give the staff regular feedback about the results of your individual giving program. Anecdotal comments from visitors about the caring, expert staff are always appreciated. Keep them updated on the results of the fund-raising program. As much as possible, show tangible evidence of what the money has been used for.

Q: *How do we arrive at our ideal generic Point of Entry event format?*

A: Take the time to experiment with various Point of Entry event formats and venues. Try having some in the morning, some late in the day or in the evening. Vary the location. If you have several program sites, you may need to try out which one works best. Once you arrive at the ideal Point of Entry event for your organization, do not change it. The more generic it is, the better.

CHAPTER 10

THE EMOTIONAL
HOOK

Of the three key ingredients for a Point of Entry event—the Facts, the Emotional Hook and a system for Capturing the Names of your guests—the Emotional Hook is the golden nugget. That is because without it, you will never develop lifelong donors.

It has been said that individuals are emotional donors looking for rational reasons to justify their emotional decision to give. So if someone comes to your Point of Entry event, and you dazzle them with the Facts alone, they probably won't be moved enough to give. They will lump your organization in with all the other nonprofits doing good work. They may walk away impressed and even a bit inspired, but they are not likely to be hooked. All the facts in the world cannot get us to give our biggest gift.

Something has got to pull at our heartstrings. If your Point of Entry event is the standard, formal presentation that people are accustomed to, they will sense it right away. You want them to know from the minute they walk up to the front door that this place is different. The Emotional Hook tells them that you really mean it about your mission. It tells you are absolutely passionate about your work.

You will need to model that passion for them. Passion is what they want from your Point of Entry event. It is okay to rant and rave a little so they get a sense of your passion. Let them know what you stand for. Perhaps even share a personal story about why you are doing the work you are doing. Most of all, you want your Point of Entry guests to leave knowing you are passionate about your work. If you can connect them to that passion, you will have gotten the job done.

In the high-tech magazine *Fast Company*, October 1999, Rolf Jensen, futurist and business strategist said:

"As information and intelligence become the domain of computers, society will place new value on the one human emotion that can't be automated: emotion. Companies will thrive on the basis of their…ability to create products and services that evoke emotion. Consumers will engage in 'emotional jogging.' They'll give their feelings a workout by using products and services that satisfy their desire to feel and display emotion."

Your job then is to figure out the Emotional Hook for your organization and to integrate it responsibly into every single communication your organization has with friends and donors, beginning with the Point of Entry event. You need to be a walking Emotional Hook for people. Most of your organization's supporters will not wake up each morning thinking about your good work. You will be their reminder, their trigger. Once they have been to your Point of Entry event, they will be counting on you to reconnect them to those same powerful emotions you triggered the first time.

Do you know what those emotions are? Can you presence them for yourself, at any moment, so as to insure every donor or potential donor who comes in contact with you will be guaranteed a dose of that Emotional Hook?

Every Organization Has an Emotional Hook

Some of you may be concerned that your organization doesn't have such a hook. After all, you are doing broad-based policy work in an obscure area, several layers removed from the grass-roots level. People don't really understand your work, let alone become emotional about it. Do not worry.

Whether your organization is a national or international think tank, a scientific professional association, or a children's hospital, every single nonprofit organization has an Emotional Hook.

Passion Retread—Tell Your Story

A good place to begin looking for your Emotional Hook is by asking yourself what got you involved with your organization in the first place. Whether you started there because you needed a job or because you were certain this was your life's work, at some point along the way, you became hooked.

It is worth looking at your story, or better yet, telling your story. In the work we do with people in our workshops to reveal the Emotional Hook of their organization, we start this "passion retread" work with the staff and volunteers.

For those who work day-to-day on the front lines, what seems like being emotionally cold or dispassionate may be natural self-preservation. At a training session for executive directors of 50 sexual assault and domestic violence organizations where we were refining the Emotional Hook, people spoke in jargon and abbreviations. When I asked them to define their terms, I was speechless. "These kinds of things actually happen to people? To children?" I stuttered. "Absolutely unthinkable."

They were concerned that if they zeroed in on their Emotional Hook, it would mean they would have to reveal confidential information. "All you have to do is define one of those terms, without ever mentioning a client's name," I said, "and people will get the message." Having them share their own stories about why they worked in this field was powerful. It returned them to their passion for their work which, understandably in many cases, had been buried for years.

Similarly, a professional association of scientists, seemingly interested only in statistics, formulas, and arcane experiments, came alive when translating their passion for their work into a simplified, lay-person's language I could understand. In several cases they were moved to tears by telling their stories of how they came to work in this field and what keeps them so engaged.

One group of hospital development staff I coached was getting ready to launch their biggest annual campaign ever. For several of the staff, it would be their 10th or even 20th annual campaign with this organization. They were hardened to the realities of life during campaign time, and already dreading it. We put aside the agenda for our session and instead went around the room, with each person telling the story of how they had come to work at this organization in the first place. It was incredibly moving. They had never done this before. In the space of an hour, the entire mood altered. One by one, you could see them "re-up" for the campaign, renewed and re-energized, ready to go.

This also works well for long-standing board and volunteers. It is a great exercise at retreats and planning sessions. It does not need to be overly gushy. Just have people tell their stories. It will reconnect them to their larger reasons for being there. And it is a terrific lead-in exercise to customizing the Emotional Hook for your organization. If what you are after is to connect people to their own emotional response to your work, you have got to start by being reconnected to what hooks *you* about it. If you are not moved, how can you expect anyone else to be?

Discovering and Customizing Your Organization's Emotional Hook

The Emotional Hook for your organization may be more subtle than you expect. It is not a tag line, an icon or a logo. It is the rallying cry and driving force behind your organization, what really stirs people up about your cause. You may never say it out loud, yet it is the underpinning of everything you say.

The Emotional Hook we are after here is not the more obvious "external hook" you talk about openly when you tell your story: the sick child, the substance-abusing mom. What we are looking for here is the "internal hook." It may not be something you ever say out loud. It usually is not pretty. It certainly may not be politically correct. Yet, when you hear it, you will recognize it as familiar because it is what you know is always present, though unspoken, in the minds of the people who come to your Point of Entry events.

It is what triggers in them the most basic human emotions, emotions like guilt, anger, fear, sadness, joy, pride. It returns us to our most cherished values. It reminds us why we care so much. It ennobles us, makes us feel larger and capable of making a real difference. At an almost subconscious level, before we realize what has happened, this internal Emotional Hook has us saying or thinking: "That's not right, it shouldn't be that way." "This is disturbing to me." "My mother or father wouldn't approve." "We must change this."

Perhaps it is our sense of injustice—"It's just not fair that gay teenagers should be shunned like that"—or that sense of rescuing someone from a terrible fate, or the fear of what will happen if we don't take action on that environmental issue now.

You arrive at this internal Emotional Hook for your organization by working with five elements:

1. The basic human emotions most stirred up by your work
2. The cherished cultural values, rights and ideals your organization addresses
3. People's deeply-held stereotypes about your work or the people you serve
4. People's hopes and dreams for how much better the world would be if the mission of your organization were fulfilled
5. Your rallying cry

Let's examine each of these critical components one by one.

Basic Human Emotions

Think of the most basic human feelings: fear, anger, sadness, joy, guilt, grief, hope, pity. These emotions are so fundamental, they often remain unconscious. They are usually stirred up before we ever speak of them.

Fear can be one of the most powerful of these emotions: Fear of what kind of water my grandchildren and great-grandchildren will be drinking, fear of contracting a particular disease, fear of a bad person harming me or my family. And don't overlook guilt or pity. It is fairly safe to assume that once people learn the facts about your work or the statistics of the incidence of your issue, they will feel guilty for not having known those facts, done more about the issue, or even cared. Before they have time to read your brochure and tell you their response, they are feeling embarrassed and guilty about their ignorance.

Remember, these are not things you will ever say out loud. Merely being aware that your organization triggers these emotions in people will make you much more effective in your fund raising. You will want to make sure that your Points of Entry trigger those emotions every time.

Cherished Cultural Values, Rights, and Ideals

Think about the services your organization provides and the people who ultimately benefit from your work. Which closely-held, cherished cultural values, rights and ideals does your work stir up in people?

For example, if your organization provides a range of services to homeless children, some of the values would be: the value of a safe and healthy childhood, the value of family, the value of a home, the value of education. If you work in the healthcare field, you are stirring up our cultural ideal of living a long, healthy life, the ideal that says no sick person should be turned away from a hospital, the value that says parents have a responsibility to take care of their children.

If you work in the area of domestic violence, you are dealing with people's values about safety, the rights of women and children, the value of family. In international relief work, you are dealing with the value that says those who have plenty should help those who have less, the value that says people deserve a chance for a better life. Other rights an organization's work might trigger are the right to privacy, to religious freedom, to education, and so on.

These are values we take for granted. They are so much a part of our way of life, we may not normally think about them. Yet, if one of those values is tampered with, we become deeply disturbed. "It is not right" that children should be treated like that. "It is unthinkable" that in a society like ours, certain conditions still prevail. Take the time to consider what cherished cultural values, rights and ideals your organization deals with.

Stereotypes

Now, look at the issues or population your organization or program deals with. What are the bleakest stereotypes people have about "those kinds of people" or those issues?

To get you going, just read through the list below and notice the stereotypes that immediately come to mind:

homeless men	political campaign reform
homeless women	world hunger
homeless children	earthquake survivors
suburban kids with learning disabilities	New York
inner-city kids with learning disabilities	California
orphans in Brazil	government employees
baby girls in China	high-tech entrepreneurs
environmentalists	private schools
symphony orchestra	debate club
art museum board	hockey team

Our stereotypes are lying around dormant, waiting to be triggered by the mere thought of your issue or the population you are committed to serving.

The best way to zero in on the stereotypes people associate with your organization is to get a group of "outsiders" to help you paint the bleakest scenario possible of the stereotypes your organization dredges up. Most people think they already know the worst. In fact, there is usually more to go.

People, even good people like us, have some pretty nasty stereotypes that underlie our actions. Take, for example, homeless "street" youth. The list of stereotypes is long: scary, worthless, already losers, it's their own fault, drug addicts, prostitutes, dropouts, dangerous, and so on. Our stereotypes call forth our smaller, petty selves. They are loaded with "shoulds." They allow us to justify the problem by saying: "They deserve it." "They brought this problem on themselves." "What difference could I make anyway? That problem will never go away."

Imagine

At the other extreme from the stereotypes is what we call the "imagine," where you imagine how life would be for all our society if the mission of your organization were fulfilled. You will definitely want to have some "outsiders" there to help you with this part. If you are a staff member, it is best to assume that you have become resigned and jaded about this. The fresh and idealistic perspective of regular folks out there in the world will be a welcome addition to this process.

What if that intractable problem you are working on were eradicated, or at least became preventable? What if no more youth were homeless? What if Internet access was available in every school? What if your researchers found the cure for that disease we most dread?

The "imagine" calls forth our expansive, generous, noble selves. It says: "That's not right." "That's not okay with me." "It shouldn't be that way." "They don't deserve that." "It's not fair." What if that intractable problem didn't have to exist anymore? It leaves us indignant, saying "We've got to do something about this!"

For the "street youth," some of the "imagines" might be: "Imagine if every child were wanted by their family." "Imagine if parents weren't abusing children." "Imagine if people understood why some youth see life on the street as better than life at home." "Imagine a society where people understood and cared about children and were capable of raising them in a loving home."

Your Rallying Cry

If there were one thing you could tell the world about your organization's work or the people you serve, what would it be? If, for one moment, you could shake them and look them in the eye, and tell them the one thing you've never been able to say before, what would you say? That is your rallying cry.

It may be "We're not kidding!" or "It's the least you can do." For many groups, the rallying cry is "You don't even have a clue," or "Pay now or pay later," or "They are smarter than you think." Perhaps your rallying cry is as simple as "We can't do this without you" or "We really need you."

What most groups see as they discover their rallying cry is the extent to which they have been holding back in conveying the real emotion of their work. This is what your donors are hungry for.

Your Hook

Now put all of this into a statement or two that boils down the essence of the Emotional Hook. For many organizations, the rallying cry alone will do. The Emotional Hook is the central statement that immediately returns *you* to the emotional essence of your work. It is your organization's internal mantra.

This is not something you will ever write in these same words in your newsletter or use as part of your public relations program. This is not the picture of the starving child. This is what lies underneath the obvious. The Emotional Hook is what it is

about *seeing* that picture—the unspoken heart of the matter—
that will hook people's emotions every time.

It may be a phrase like:

> We save children here. Young helpless children who cannot speak
> up for themselves. This should not ever have to happen to
> another child. Ever.

or

> Imagine if your great grandchildren would never know what it
> is like to take a hike in the woods.

That's why we call it the Emotional Hook. Because it hooks
you. And that is where you need to start to be able to hook *them*.

Applying the Hook

Once you know this internal Emotional Hook for your organization, you will want to integrate it into every single
communication you have with your donors and potential donors. You can safely assume that these people did not wake up
this morning already hooked by your work.

At your Point of Entry event, the Emotional Hook should be
brilliantly intertwined with the Facts about your work—the statistics, those good appease-the-mind sound bites we all need,
your photos, the testimonials, and case examples you show. All
these should trigger the Emotional Hook. Every issue of your
newsletter, every invitation, every phone call, mailing or email,
should contain some vestige of the Emotional Hook. Donors
are counting on you to make it present every time they come in
contact with you. You and your organization are their reminder
system for this critical issue. Do not back off.

Always, the message you are trying to convey is "This work
changes lives." No matter how abstract, how far-removed from
the day-to-day lives of the people who will ultimately benefit,
you wouldn't be doing this work if you didn't believe it will,
sooner or later, improve life for regular people. You must keep
saying that. Boil it all down to the life of one family, one child,

one villager. That is the only way people can get their hands around your issue. Make it human scale. Tell us how life will be better. Give us specific examples that trigger the Emotional Hook.

Finally, you have to be responsible about your organization's internal Emotional Hook. You do not want to overdo it. Too much of an Emotional Hook can leave people feeling manipulated and embarrassed. You don't want them to direct their anger towards you! You want them to be angry and riled up about your issue, so they will want to support you in dealing effectively with the problem. Sometimes subtlety is better. Allude to the Emotional Hook, know that you have made your point and then leave it alone.

On the other hand, don't diminish the Emotional Hook. It is a legitimate and powerful tool at your disposal. People will have emotional reactions to your work whether or not you plan for them to have those reactions. Once you know what those Emotional Hooks are, manage them responsibly. Use them to steer people in the direction of taking action.

By all means, resist any temptation to shrink back to presenting your organization as the meek and struggling nonprofit trying to do good work, fighting the good fight. You have to be responsible for how important your work is, for what a difference it is making and will continue to make. You have to be genuinely moved by the work and unafraid to convey that.

You have to believe and let your donors know you believe. Ultimately, if you don't reach in and hook their hearts, they won't remember you for long. You will be just one more needy cause rather than their personal cause. You want them to discover for themselves that your organization is worthy of their fullest contribution. That is what you are after.

CHAPTER II

TREASURE MAPS—
WHO TO INVITE TO A
POINT OF ENTRY

As you begin to see the merit of Points of Entry events, you will naturally wonder who to invite to come to them. Given the person-to-person nature of this model, it only makes sense to start with the people who already are connected to you in some way. You can branch out from there, following the stream of passion and natural word-of-mouth that links people. Before you know it, the whole system will snowball.

Rather than spending time trying to interest the obvious wealthy donors in your community who may not know or care about your organization, take the time to brainstorm the natural supporters who are lurking right under your nose. I use the term Treasure Map because it identifies the natural treasure around you right now. You don't have to go out of your way to find these people. You don't have to make your selections based on wealth or social status. Include everyone and brainstorm away.

Learning to Draw a Treasure Map

This is a brainstorming exercise that is best done with a group of people who are all committed to producing the same result, such as inviting people to Points of Entry events or deciding whom to involve in any project or event you are working on.

The first time you use the Treasure Map, I recommend you walk through the steps on your own, preferably with a large piece of paper and some colored markers. Later in this chapter we will talk about how to use this exercise with a group.

Begin by drawing a circle in the center of the page. Put the name of your organization in the circle.

Then surround your organization, like the spokes on a wheel, with all the other groups you come in contact with on a regular basis. Start with groups like your board, staff, volunteers, donors and funders, vendors, and other groups in the community that you interact with regularly.

**Treasure Map
Groups & Organizations©**

Resources in Abundance

Now, with a different colored pen or marker, list the resources which each of these groups has in abundance. Why? Because this is an abundance-based model of fund raising. It presumes people will naturally want to give that which they have plenty of.

Most of us do not like saying no; it makes us feel mean and uncaring. People would much rather say yes when you ask them. It is much easier for them to say yes if you are asking them to give you something you know they already have in excess. For some people, you may not know what that is, but it usually doesn't take long to find out when you think about whom you could ask.

So go back to the Treasure Map you have begun and start listing out the abundant resources of your board, staff, volunteers, etc. For example, your board might have an abundance of passion, commitment, expertise, contacts, and money. Your volunteers might have an abundance of time, expertise, connections, and money as well. How about your staff? They have an abundance of passion, first-hand stories about the good work of your organization, time (because they are being paid for their time at work), and expertise. Take the time to do this with each group. What resources do they have in abundance?

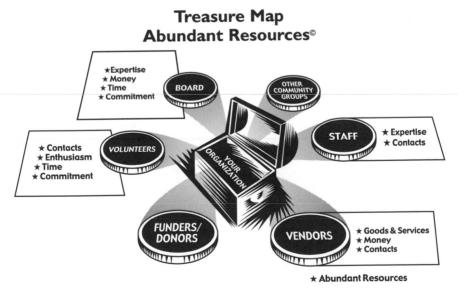

Treasure Map
Abundant Resources©

Self Interest

Next, go back over each group and ask what their self-interest would be in coming to your Point of Entry event. What is the value or benefit for them in attending?

Let's pause a minute to talk about self-interest. As we said earlier, self-interest is a good thing. It drives everything we do. For example, you have a definite self-interest in reading this book. Maybe that self-interest is finding new ideas, maybe it is pleasing the boss, or maybe it is because you wanted a break from your work. Self-interest is always there, and, as a person who is interested in raising funds, you should think of it as a very useful resource.

Self-interest can range from the most negative and selfish motives all the way to the most noble and inspiring. Consider the full range of self-interest as you go back to your Treasure Map and list the self-interests of each group.

Consider, for example, your donors or funders. What benefit does being connected to you have for them? Ask yourself, "What is in this for them?" Yes, they may want a tax write-off, but this is rarely the sole reason for making a gift. For most donors, a major self-interest is feeling good about making the gift and feeling they are making a difference. For some donors, self-interest is paying back someone for something they once received. Or maybe they have a personal connection to the services you offer. Or they feel that giving to your organization is a kind of insurance, that what you are committed to preventing won't happen to them. Guilt can be a self-interest, so can impressing others and looking good. Maybe they are giving because they want to have a child or grandchild accepted into your private school or college.

Look at the self-interest of your volunteers. Why are they involved with you? Perhaps it is to make a difference, to contribute their talents, to learn new skills, to build their resume for their next job, to give back, to keep busy, and on and on. What about your board? For some, their self-interest is to please a boss who "asked" them to serve on your board. For others, it is a personal connection, a way of giving back, or a feel-good thing. Some are so henpecked at work that serving on a board lets them feel important.

Donor by donor, self-interest is a key driver of your self-sustaining, individual giving program. Whatever your donors' self interests, the sooner you know them, the easier it will be to customize your fund-raising program to their needs.

Treasure Map
Self Interests©

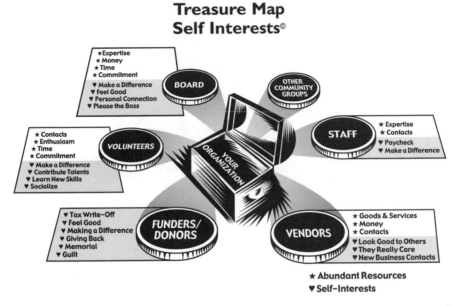

★ Abundant Resources
♥ Self-Interests

Self-interest is more complex than it appears at first. If you really take the time to identify the self-interests of each group on your Treasure Map, you will shortcut your work greatly. You will be more compassionate for the folks who come to visit, and down the road, as they become lifelong donors, you will want to remember back to the self-interest that led to their involvement in the first place.

Fantasy Categories

Next, looking back at your Treasure Map, add in some fantasy categories. Who is not yet on your map that you would love to have? Whose involvement would leverage a whole world of support and credibility? Add those people to your Treasure Map, too. Some typical fantasy categories include celebrities, athletes, corporate executives, and media figures. For some organizations, having the support of a local opinion leader, a religious leader, or an expert on your issue, could quickly leverage your story into the larger community.

Let yourself play with this one. This is why it is fun to do a Treasure Map with a group of people.

Treasure Map Fantasy Groups©

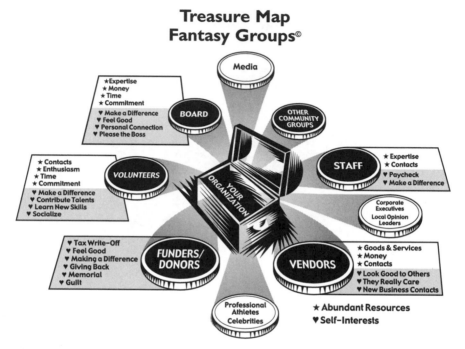

Media

★Expertise
★ Money
★ Time
★ Commitment

♥ Make a Difference
♥ Feel Good
♥ Personal Connection
♥ Please the Boss

BOARD

OTHER COMMUNITY GROUPS

★ Contacts
★ Enthusiasm
★ Time
★ Commitment

♥ Make a Difference
♥ Contribute Talents
♥ Learn New Skills
♥ Socialize

VOLUNTEERS

YOUR ORGANIZATION

STAFF

★ Expertise
★ Contacts

♥ Paycheck
♥ Make a Difference

Corporate Executives
Local Opinion Leaders

♥ Tax Write-Off
♥ Feel Good
♥ Making a Difference
♥ Giving Back
♥ Memorial
♥ Guilt

FUNDERS/ DONORS

VENDORS

★ Goods & Services
★ Money
★ Contacts

♥ Look Good to Others
♥ They Really Care
♥ New Business Contacts

Professional Athletes Celebrities

★ Abundant Resources
♥ Self-Interests

Connecting the Groups

Finally, draw the connecting lines between those groups on your Treasure Map who already talk to each other. You will see instantly how fast news travels. If a handful of people come to your sizzling Point of Entry event, who will they tell?

If your staff talks to your volunteers, draw a connecting line between those two groups. If your board and vendors talk only occasionally, you might draw a dotted line. For those groups who don't talk to each other at all, draw no connecting lines. The connections will vary for each organization. It is worth taking the time to go through this one category at a time. It can spark many insights.

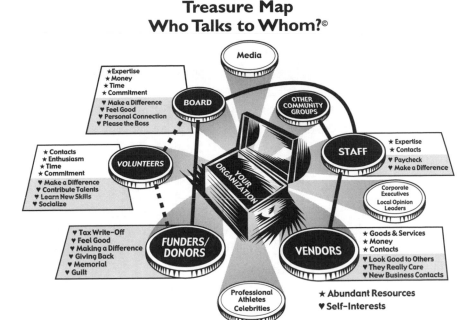

Treasure Map
Who Talks to Whom?©

There you have it, your first Treasure Map. Now let's look at how to apply it to your organization.

Creating a Treasure Map with Your Organization

The Treasure Map exercise is most effective if done in a group. As with most brainstorming exercises, the more people who participate in the process, the more creativity will spring forth and the more people will be likely to buy into making something happen down the road.

As an example, let's look at doing the Treasure Map exercise with your board or a subgroup of your board, the development committee. Here is how you might use the Treasure Map to generate a list of people to invite to your Points of Entry events.

First, be sure you are comfortable doing the exercise yourself before taking it to the board. You might try it out with a smaller, safer group of staff the first couple of times, or even with family or friends. One or two practices should do it; just be sure you feel comfortable with the exercise before you lead your board through it.

Then, armed with your flip chart and colored markers, stand up and guide the board through the process of constructing the Treasure Map, step by step. Begin with the name of your organization in the center. Add the groups you naturally come in contact with, their resources, their self-interests, the fantasy groups you would love to count as treasure, and finally, add the lines which show you who talks to whom. Let the board call out their responses as you write them down.

Next, give each board member a blank piece of paper and have them make a Treasure Map for themselves personally. People put their own names in the middle. Then have them go through the same steps of adding the groups they naturally come in contact with, what each group has in abundance, the self-interests of the groups in coming to a Point of Entry event for your organization, their fantasy groups, and the lines connecting those who know each other. Give them enough time to get into doing the exercise. They probably will be surprised by all the treasure they have.

Now, reconvene the group as a whole and make a new collective Treasure Map for the entire board. Put "Art Museum Board" in the middle. Then let them call out the groups they all saw that they naturally interact with. They will have many of the same categories: business associates, friends, family, neighbors, religious organizations, church group, children's school or sports groups, pals from the gym or the golf club, book club, college alumni association, sororities, etc. Get them up there on the diagram. The chart will be impressive.

Next, assuming the board has already attended the "demo, kick-the-tires" Point of Entry event and they know what you are talking about, you can ask them to look back to their personal Treasure Maps and make a list of 10 to 20 individuals they would feel comfortable inviting.

Give them the dates of the next Point of Entry events and ask how many people they would commit to having there. You can even give them pre-stamped postcard invitations to the next Point of Entry event that they can personalize and mail after their guests have been invited by phone.

Don't be discouraged if you don't get 100% participation. Just focus on the people who want to play the game. The others will come along later, once they see the results.

Treasure Map Interviews

If people are reluctant to invite others to a Point of Entry event right away or if they feel the people on their list might need a bit more warming up, you might suggest they start with a Treasure Map Interview.

Treasure Map Interviews are a powerful tool for eliciting open-ended feedback about your organization. The interviews are also invaluable for reconnecting with prior or current friends of the organization, including people who might be upset with the organization for one reason or another. As you build your self-sustaining, individual-giving program, you will see many uses for Treasure Map Interviews.

In the Raising More Money workshops, participants are assigned to interview at least 10 people from their Treasure Maps, just to see the value of conducting this type of open-ended dialog. In particular, if the person is new to their organization, the Treasure Map Interviews are an ideal way to quickly connect to all the key players. This is strictly an information gathering interview. You are not, in any way, asking for money. You are not even hinting about asking for money. At this point, you are on a mission to gather their thoughts, their opinions, and their advice as it pertains to your organization.

These interviews are all about listening. Forget the clipboard and the checklist of closed-ended questions designed to lead the potential donor to give you the responses you want to hear. These questions are truly open-ended. You can have fun with them and let them lead you wherever they may. When people come back to class to report on having done the interviews, many say this was the single, most important thing they have done. Just learning to be quiet and listen to people as they pour out their hearts and opinions is an essential skill in the new reality.

Likewise, you do not need to schedule a formal interview time to conduct a Treasure Map Interview, unless you prefer to do so. You can work these questions into your normal conversations with people. Remember, if the people you will be interviewing are on your Treasure Map, they are most likely people you see or talk to from time to time anyway.

It is fine to ask them the interview questions while you are driving somewhere together, having lunch, or attending a meeting. I often recommend workshop participants start by interviewing someone close to them who is "easy," such as a spouse or partner, child or parent, neighbor or close friend. Often, the people closest to us have plenty of thoughts and opinions about our organizations, we just never think to ask them. For some, another easy first interview can be done with a stranger on a bus or airplane.

Here are the suggested Treasure Map Interview questions to get you going. You do not need to use them all. Once you get the hang of this, you will be able to modify and tailor them to your own style and situation. You may select different questions for different people you interview.

Treasure Map Interview Questions

1. What do you know about our organization?

2. What images come to mind when you think of us?

   You may be surprised to learn that even if they have never heard of your organization before, there will be certain images that come to mind anyway.

3. How did you come to know about us or become involved with us?

Let them take as long as they would like to tell you their story.

4. What do you like about being a friend of our organization?

You may be pleasantly surprised by all the nice things people have to say. Note which things matter most to them.

5. Where or how do you think we are really missing the boat?

Notice your tendency to become defensive here. Put yourself in their shoes. These may be things they have been harboring for awhile—things they really do want to communicate. If they sense that you are trying to justify or make excuses in any way, they will back off. You will not have gathered the critical feedback you are seeking. Resist the temptation to talk at all. Just be quiet and listen.

6. What advice do you have for us?

Regardless of how well they know you, they will have advice for you. Everyone loves giving advice.

7. What cues might we have missed from you?

You might hear things like: "After all the years I've been sending in those $100 checks, I'm surprised no one called to ask me to give more."

8. How could we tell our story better?

People often say things like: "I wish you'd stop sending me those long boring newsletters. I only like the part with the stories about the people you've helped."

9. What could we do to involve more people?

This is where people often suggest names of others you should call. Or they may offer to help you connect with the person in charge of arranging speakers for a particular business group. If you have done a good job of listening up until now, the person will definitely be forthcoming with suggestions.

Remember, the Treasure Map Interviews have no hidden agenda. You are not trying to get anyone to give you anything. Your only objective is to listen carefully to the other person's responses.

At the end of the interview, be sure to thank them sincerely for their time. Jot down what they actually said, not your thoughts and opinions about what they said. Also write down any next steps that may be needed based on the input you received. Be sure these notes are kept in your data base, which should have a "notes" section for each person you interview.

Additional Uses for the Treasure Map Interviews

The Treasure Map Interview is a powerful tool for deepening your connection to your donors and potential donors in an open-ended, non-threatening way. If you actually do the interviews, if you take the time to really listen, people will tell you everything you need to know about precisely how they would like to be involved. You may notice people talking themselves into becoming more involved with you, just in the process of the interview.

Here are a number of ways Treasure Map Interviews can be used:

1. As an easy lead-in for board and volunteers who have done the Treasure Map exercise to engage people in their lives in an initial dialog about your organization. Often, by the end of the interview, the person will want to know more. It may be very natural, at that point, to invite them to one of your upcoming Point of Entry tours or box-lunch introductory sessions. Rather than "hitting them cold" with the invitation, you will be responding to their interest in becoming connected or reconnected to your organization.

2. As follow-up questions after your happy Multiple-Year Donors have come to a Free Feel-Good Cultivation Event (Chapter 22). Each event begins another series of one-on-one follow-up contact. To deepen their relationship with you, you can choose a few questions from the list to find

out more about the interests and concerns of your Multiple-Year Donors. Use that Follow-Up Call to elicit their open-ended thoughts and listen closely for the rich cues they will be giving you.

3. To quickly get acquainted with all the key players if you are new to your organization or position. Imagine your accelerated learning curve if you took the time to interview a few people from each group on your organization's Treasure Map: the board, staff, donors, and clients. Do not limit yourself. Interview everyone!

4. To reconnect with people who might be upset with your organization for one reason or another. Even if it has been several years since someone spoke to this person, it is never too late. These people are well worth the effort. At some point in the past, they put their heart and soul into some aspect of your work. For whatever reason, they left unhappy or unsatisfied. They do not want to hold a grudge forever. They need to be heard. They need you to listen and perhaps take some action. I have heard countless stories of former board members, donors, and volunteers coming back into the organization's family after someone took the time to do a Treasure Map Interview with them. Remember, every one of these people has the potential to become a lifelong major donor.

5. To reconnect with people with whom your organization has gotten a bit out of touch. Time goes by, people are busy, and before you know it, it may have been two or three years since you have spoken with those cherished former board members, founders and former donors. In these situations, an apology may be necessary before you ask permission to launch into a few questions. We will talk more about this in Chapter 13 when we discuss the Cultivation Superhighway.

6. In a Know-thy-Donor "Thankathon," where your core team of board members, staff, and volunteers is calling loyal donors personally, often for the first time. After you have

thanked them for their support over the years and told them you are overdue in asking for their input, ask a few of the Treasure Map Interview questions, customized to your situation. This can lead into inviting them to a Point of Entry event or a special Point of Re-Entry event designed for donors at their giving level. This will be discussed more in Chapter 22.

Now we are ready to move on to Step Two in our model.

CHAPTER 12

STEP TWO:
FOLLOW UP AND
INVOLVE

Follow Up is Step Two in our model, the step many people say is the most important. When you are looking to build life-long donors, the follow-up process never ends. After the initial Point of Entry event, as well as after every subsequent event, you will want to be in contact with your key donors asking for their personal feedback.

If you think of this as a systematic research call, the Follow-Up Call can provide you with the personalized input you will need about each potential donor. What will it take to have them feel they have made a real contribution? To what extent do they want to become involved? Then you will need to customize a plan or pathway for that particular donor.

Much of the current business marketing research tells us that the sooner you can talk to the customer first-hand and ask them their preferences and opinions, the sooner you can give them what they want and keep them coming back for more. As a result, many businesses design elaborate strategies to have a legitimate reason to talk to their customers.

In our model, however, the Point of Entry event easily sets up the Follow-Up Call. As your guests are leaving the Point of Entry event—inspired, informed, armed with your literature and rushing off to their next appointment—the person who will be doing the Follow-Up Call says to each of them: "Thank you for coming. I'll give you a call later this week to get your feedback."

Who Makes the Follow-Up Call?

Before you launch into implementing this model, it is worth thinking through who will be responsible for making the Follow-Up Calls. A personal, one-to-one relationship model requires talking to people on a regular basis. Who is the right person to be doing the communicating and recording the feedback?

I recommend you choose the most senior-ranking person you can spare who is able to attend all the Point of Entry events, since you only want Follow-Up Calls to be made by a person whom the guest met at the event. The caller needs to be someone who has a direct line to the head of the organization, someone with maturity, "people skills," and outstanding organizational skills. It needs to be someone who can screen the many good ideas people will have for you, and someone with the authority to act on them or to pull together the decision makers who can act quickly. A donor or potential donor with a hot idea expects and deserves immediate attention.

If you decide to have more than one person responsible for Follow Up, be sure they share a computer data base and update each other regularly. You might want to assign each of them to be the Donor Service Representative for their own group of donors so that those donors feel they have their own contact person.

The Script for Your Follow-Up Calls

The Follow-Up Call is not just a courteous thank-you call, in which case a note would suffice. Think of this as a research call with a specific script of points to be covered. You are a detective on a mission to determine how each person might like to become involved, even if only a little bit, with your organization. It has to be a custom-fitted type of involvement, tailored to their needs and interests. You must have your radar detector turned up to high intensity for this call. You are listening for cues.

The better you listen, the more you will hear exactly how they might want to become involved. Involvement is what you are after, and listening is the key. You may need to practice asking people questions and then not talking so you can really zero in on the essence of their response—as well as what they are not saying.

Here is a suggested script for the Follow-Up Call, including the points to be covered:

Point 1: Hello, Maria. You may remember me from the tour at the children's home last week. I was calling to *thank you for taking the time to come out and visit us.* It means a great deal to us that you took your time to do that.

As we said last week, we are having these tours as a way to tell our story to more people in the community, to expand the base of folks who know what we're doing. We'd really appreciate your feedback.

Point 2: *What did you think* of the tour?

Now pause and let them talk as long as they like. As you are listening closely to their response, pick up on any cues or hot buttons that interest them. Add a bit more information about programs they like. If they don't offer anything more, and they have not told you that they absolutely are not interested, you can proceed to the next question.

Point 3: *Is there any way you could see yourself becoming involved with our organization?*

Notice in their response what kind of involvement they are looking for. Is it something very hands-on and tangible? A project, perhaps? An in-kind donation? Or do they prefer more of an arms-length advisory or referral role? All of these qualify as involvement.

People don't like to say no. They want to be nice to you. They want to help you. They also want to get you off their backs. So, you have to listen carefully to read the signals. If they are not interested—no way, no how—just thank them again and say goodbye. In the long run, they will respect you a lot more for respecting their time and involvement in other organizations. Many times, they will send you their friends who truly are interested in your work.

The last question, if they haven't already offered:

Point 4: *Is there anyone else you would suggest we invite to another introductory (Point of Entry) event like the one you attended?*

If they give you a name, ask, "Would it be all right for me to call them and mention your name, or would you prefer to call the person first to let them know I will be calling?"

Any suggestions, names, or ideas they have given you need to be acted on immediately and, in turn, reported back to them quickly.

Rethinking Your Definition of "Donor"

As you may already have suspected, this model requires that you let go of the "old reality" roles for donors in your organization and do some new-reality soul searching.

Are you truly willing to have donors get involved in ways that are meaningful to *them* as well as you? That is what today's donors are asking for. If they are going to become lifelong members of your family, they want to know that you value their input, that they can call you up and have a frank conversation with you, that you will call them once in awhile for their input.

Let's stop for a minute and consider this picture from the donor's point of view.

Imagine yourself as one of the guests at your organization's Point of Entry event—a tour, a reception, a box lunch informational meeting. You attend one event and you were impressed. You could see that this organization is right on the mark.

Now what? They didn't ask you for money. They sent you home with some materials. You take a minute to read them. How interesting. There is an easy-to-read Wish List of all kinds of things they need. There are little items like toothbrushes, shampoo, pots and pans, help in the office once a week. And there are some medium-sized items like old computers, carpeting for the youth room, a van, math tutors. The list goes all the way up to the really big stuff: a new gymnasium, an underwriter for their international conference, a new office building, a properly-staffed reading program.

You see that you could actually contribute some of the things on that list, but you are too busy to pick up the phone and call them or you might not want to appear that "forward." You put away the Wish List and go on to the next activity in your day.

Two days later, you get a phone call from that nice staff person you met at the tour or lunch meeting. She is thanking you for taking your time to come and asking for your input. "What did you think of our program?" You tell her in a reserved way how impressed you were. You mention that the intercultural studies program was especially appealing. At some point, she asks: "Is there any way you could see yourself becoming involved?"

You may be thinking about underwriting that international conference. After all, it links to many other interests of yours, yet you don't want to lead off with something so big. "I notice you need some old computers," you respond. "I could help you with that."

She is very appreciative and tells you immediately how much they are needed and for which program. The demand has increased so much that the computer lab is now open every evening and there are still people who can't get the computer time they need. My goodness, you are thinking, my old computers could really make a difference. We've upgraded our system at the office and those old ones are actually in the way. I'd be a real hero if I found a good cause to donate them to.

"Would it help if we came to pick them up?" she offers. "I know how happy it will make the people in the computer lab to have them before the new round of classes start." Next thing you know, they have picked up the computers and you are getting a call inviting you to come back and see the expanded computer program in action one evening when it is in full swing. "Feel free to invite anyone else you'd like," offers that same warm, efficient staff person.

You arrive with your husband and two work colleagues just to check it out on your way to dinner. You are dazzled. Those old computers that had been cluttering the back room at the office are now front and center, with eager, curious children and their parents clicking away. The head of the computer program, a brainy-looking fellow, happens to be there in the midst of all the action. He can't thank you enough.

Of course, as part of the evening's show-and-tell of the computer center, your low-key guide points out the students from the intercultural program, communicating with their international "e-pals". "It's just a start," she says, "they're always hungry for more real connections with other cultures." You go off to dinner with your friends. Everyone is feeling good and you are looking like the person of the hour. For your friends, this was a Point of Entry event; for you it was a validation that you picked a winner.

The next week, the same nice staff person calls back to thank you for coming out again and for bringing those friends. "What did they think of it?" she asks. "Do you think they'd have any interest in getting involved? Would it be all right with you if I give them a call? Is there any more you would like in the way of information or involvement?"

And so it goes. A one-time visit to a Point of Entry event and an effective Follow-Up Call lead to more and more.

A few points to consider:

- Are you making your needs known to first-time, potential contributors?

- Do you have a Wish List with a wide array of items you'd really love to have? Could you link each item to a staff person or department that would be thrilled to receive them?

- If someone chooses to get involved on a volunteer basis, are you prepared to take care of them to insure a super-positive experience?

- What if they identify an area of interest that you've never thought of? Are you flexible enough to think it through together?

Today's potential donors want to get involved in meaningful ways. They want to call the shots. They want to control the pace of their relationship with you. They are prepared to be loyal. They are always testing to be sure you really need them. They appreciate an honest answer more than an obvious, polite response. They are looking for the perfect blend of their talents and resources with your needs. And so are you!

The Follow-Up Call is your ticket to customizing the ideal type of involvement for that donor. It is essential to building a self-sustaining, individual-giving program in the new fund-raising reality.

CHAPTER 13

DEEPENING YOUR RELATIONSHIP WITH DONORS

Once someone has come to your Point of Entry event and received a Follow-Up Call where they express some level of interest in your work, they become a potential donor. In the for-profit world, this person would be called a potential customer, and the nonprofit world has a great deal to learn from the re-search and trends in the fields of customer service and marketing.

What we do to turn that potential donor into a lifelong do-nor has everything to do with "donor service." For our purposes, you could say that donor service means listening to your poten-tial and actual donors and meeting their needs, listening to them some more and meeting those needs, then doing it again and again. Today's donors don't care what the next person says or complains about; they want their needs and concerns handled—and right now.

Rather than applying an old-reality, mass marketing strategy to all donors, the new fund-raising reality calls for customization and personalization at every level. Book titles like *One-to-One Marketing* and *One Size Fits One* tell us that we need to develop a data base on each and every person and not presume we can extrapolate any of that data to any other person. The more we can keep asking *you* what *you* want, the more we can deliver it and make *you* happy.

True Contribution

Before we can look at how this applies to our donors and potential donors, it is worth pausing to remind ourselves what it is we are aiming for. How will we know if we have succeeded? How do we engage people in precisely the ways that will have them want to give?

What we are looking for are happy, lifelong donors. Lifelong donors are people who regard your organization's work as vital and exciting. They are people for whom a gift to your organization is not just a donation, it's a real contribution.

In the old fund-raising reality, we would be scolding ourselves for not having asked for a check at the Point of Entry. That was the "strong arm-thy-Rolodex" model of Asking where the underlying, unspoken assumption was, "Someone around here knows you, therefore we have a right to ask you for money." Back then, we had short-term goals to meet. Cultivating lifelong donors was not a priority. Each successive wave of board members would solicit their friends. The old reality also presumed a bottomless pit of potential donors. Even if only a small percentage said yes, we could move on to others the next year. Our existence as nonprofit organizations was hand-to-mouth, year-to-year. Building something for the future was only a dream.

In the new reality, giving is an ongoing process of ever-deepening engagement, involvement, and permission from donors to ask them for more. There is a give-and-take which requires a depth of listening skills that was not essential before. There is a respect and honoring of each donor as an individual who is genuinely interested in contributing. There is an interest in building a long-term relationship.

To put it simply, you want to treat each donor as if they have the potential to become a major donor. Regardless of the size of your contribution, treat them with the same respect and dignity you would want to receive.

It is often helpful to begin by recalling that you, too, are a donor. Your name is on the donor list of many organizations. Think for a moment of all the places you contributed money in the past year: your kids' school or soccer team, your church, synagogue or religious organization, your professional association, your alumni association, the community hospital.

Going back over your list, notice how much money you gave to each of them. Think about the medium by which you were solicited in each case: in person, by mail, by phone, online? Look at how many years you have been giving to each of these groups. Now think about how involved you feel with each organization you give to. How much contact do they have with you in the course of a year? Is there any correlation between how involved you feel and how much you give?

Next, look at your in-kind contributions. Make a similar list of the groups or individuals you have made a non-financial contribution to in the past year. Include any charitable organization where you have given your time, your expertise, volunteered on a board, a committee, planned an event, offered advice, or just listened to a friend in need. Think again of how many hours you spent doing this, the circumstances in which you were asked to make that contribution, and how connected or involved you felt with the organization or individual you gave to. For how many months or years have you been giving there?

Looking back over all the places you have given money or in-kind gifts, ask yourself what qualities were present when you felt good about your giving? You will notice that these same qualities are usually missing when you haven't felt good about contributing.

In those cases where you felt good about your giving, you probably have felt it truly made a difference. You felt connected or involved with the cause. It related to a personal experience you had been through. You were giving back or repaying a favor or a debt of gratitude. You were memorializing a loved one.

The odds are, if it was truly a contribution rather than giving as a result of feeling manipulated or "strong armed" by someone, you weren't even looking for recognition when you did it. The giving itself was a source of personal pleasure. You felt connected in some way to the group or cause. You felt they were making good use of your contribution. You felt that whatever the size of your contribution, they needed it and appreciated it.

That is exactly the way you want your donors to feel when they give to your organization. They should feel so good about their gift they don't have to tell anyone else they did it—as if your organization is their special project, their personal indulgence.

You want them to feel as though they have sprinkled fairy dust on the most worthy organization in the world. You want them to feel as though they are an insider to your organization, as though they are a true friend or even part of the family. They will feel the way you feel when you know you have truly contributed. That's the feeling you are after. If you have accomplished that, you will have allowed them to truly contribute.

Everything you do to connect and reconnect with a potential donor after the Point of Entry is designed to deepen and enhance this sense of true contribution. That is what will develop loyal committed lifelong donors who are giving for the right reasons.

Donor Service

Now we can move on to "customer service" or what we would call Donor Service. Let's look at good, solid, "regular" customers like ourselves. It will give us more compassion for seeing things from the donor's point of view.

Think of a recent consumer experience where you as the consumer were left frustrated or upset. (Popular sources of frustration, just to get you started, are travel, computer, phone, or car problems.) Think back to that moment when you felt angry and alone. Perhaps you actually tried complaining about it, or perhaps you just stewed in silence.

If you were fortunate, the situation was resolved to your satisfaction. If it was resolved, what did it take to resolve it? If it was not resolved, what would it have taken to make you a happy customer again? Tell the truth. For many of us, money would help ease the pain—a gift certificate, a free plane ticket—or perhaps just a letter of sincere apology or knowing that they changed the system so this mistake wouldn't happen again. It is interesting to note that as customers, we want to work it out, we want to come back and be good customers again. We don't want to go away angry.

Now, think of a situation where you volunteer your time to a nonprofit organization. Perhaps you serve on a board or committee or work in an office. Or you may give time in a more direct role, helping at a school, a library, a homeless shelter. How much time do you give weekly or monthly? What frustrations do you have? What complaints do you have? What would it take to make you happy? You may give quite a bit of time to this organization, perhaps you have been volunteering for many years. Yet, even you, their happy volunteer, have frustrations and little things you put up with. You might want to contrast that to your very best volunteer or board experiences. Why are some of your volunteer experiences so much better than others?

One of my most positive experiences is as a board member of a local hospital. While many other organizations would have commented repeatedly about my poor attendance at board meetings and made me feel guilty enough to resign, this organization has inquired into my needs. They understand my travel schedule. They go out of their way to notify me early of special meetings and retreats so I can plan around them. We review together which meetings are most important to attend. They deliver reading materials for the next meeting to my door in plenty of time for me to review them while I'm on the road.

They are constantly thanking me for the time I *do* give them. Rather than making me feel guilty, they make me feel special. They have customized their approach to me and, I can only assume, they do the same for each of the other board members.

Finally, think of a recent situation in which you have been a frustrated donor. Perhaps the organization misspelled your name, got your address wrong, or botched up the processing of your gift. Maybe your name didn't make it to the correct donor level in their annual report. Or perhaps they neglected to invite you to their fancy recognition dinner, or they seated you at the wrong table, or you thought the event was too lavish and extravagant. What more could they have done to make you happy, to fix the problem, and to win you back at an even deeper level of commitment?

Looking back over all these situations—as a consumer, as a volunteer, and as a donor—what qualities of donor service were missing? What did you need that was missing? On the other hand, when you have felt served and taken care of as a customer, what qualities were present?

When we do this as an exercise in the Raising More Money workshop, people often say what they needed were things like:

- I wanted them to listen to me, to hear me out.
- I wanted them to get creative and come up with a solution that would meet my needs.
- I needed them to sincerely apologize, to show that they valued my time, to follow up in a timely manner with a real solution, to correct the problem in their system so this would not happen to someone else.
- I needed them to be honest with me. I needed to feel like I was talking to a real person, not a machine.
- I wanted to know they were going to do something about the problem, not just apologize to me. I needed to see tangible actions taken.

Today's consumers and donors are both smart and sensitive. We can sense when people are not being honest with us. Our time is valuable, and if you don't show us that you appreciate us at least as much as you appreciate the next customer, we can certainly take our business elsewhere. We have come to expect personal treatment, to expect that you will remember our preferences and won't make us tell you repeatedly what we are *not* interested in.

As you go through the process of deepening your relationship with your donors, you can assume they will have suggestions and complaints. To quote Harvard marketing guru, Theodore Levitt, "Nobody is ever that satisfied, especially not over an extended period of time." I recommend you develop the habit of asking donors and potential donors for feedback at every possible opportunity and then take that feedback seriously.

It all starts in the Follow-Up Call. If you are impersonal and perfunctory, a potential donor will conclude that your entire organization is impersonal and perfunctory. If you are warm and polite, not overstepping the limited degree of permission you have been granted to date, you may gain permission to go a bit further. If you are "real" with the person on the other end of the phone, asking a few relevant questions and then listening to the answers as if you were in the presence of true genius, you will connect with the person. You will leave them with the experience that something is different about your organization. You will reinforce the positive and moving experience they had at your Point of Entry event. You will validate that they are getting involved with a solid organization that truly values their participation.

In other words, you need to treat every donor or potential donor, from the moment they walk in the door at your Point of Entry event, as you would want to be treated. Don't be overly sweet or presumptuous. If they are a formal, more reserved person, you may need to be a bit more formal and more reserved with them. If they are laid back and convivial, you may need to loosen up a bit yourself.

The more you can stop thinking about yourself and consider their needs at the moment, the better. Ask yourself: What am I really interested in knowing about this person? What feedback would I value from them? What can I learn from this person?

The Cultivation Superhighway

In our model, the part of the circle between Step Two: Follow Up and Involve and Step Three: Asking for Money is what we call the Cultivation Superhighway. Everything that happens here between your organization and the donor or potential donor is designed to hasten the ripening of the fruit that will be ready to be picked by Step Three.

What accelerates the pace on the Cultivation Superhighway are contacts. I often tell people that individual giving is a contact sport. That is because there is a direct correlation between the number of contacts you have with a potential donor along this superhighway and the size of their gifts. The more personal contacts, the larger the gift.

This should come as no surprise. Think again about your own giving to those organizations you are most loyal to, the places you have given to for years. Think about how much contact they have with you in the course of a year. It is probably not much.

Now imagine receiving more customized contact from someone at that organization several times throughout the year: invitations to events, lectures, or parties connected to your interests and lifestyle, events that include your family, small receptions where you can talk with that noted author or researcher one-on-one. Then imagine that you have your own Donor Services Representatives, someone who personally invites you to each of these events. With each invitation, your feedback would be solicited about programs and services you would like to know more about, programs you could get more involved in. Your Donor Services Representative would get to know your preferences and interests and offer relevant suggestions.

Even if your schedule wouldn't permit you to attend any of the events, you would feel appreciated by this organization. Someone had taken the time to talk with you personally and genuinely try to serve your interests. The next time they asked you to give, you would undoubtedly say yes, probably at a higher level than before. If this customized cultivation and re-cultivation process were to continue, you would feel more and more connected, more and more trusting of the organization, and in turn, you would probably grant them more permission to ask you for more and more of your resources.

That is what it takes to build a lifelong donor, and that, after all, is what you are aiming for.

Communicating on the Cultivation Superhighway

In your interactions with every donor or potential donor, I recommend using the following template for communicating. It will deepen and authenticate the cultivation process.

1. Listen

Remember from your own experiences as a customer, volunteer or donor that one of your most basic needs is simply to be listened to and heard. As a staff member or representative of the organization, your first job in *every* communication, is to listen. Just listen. Listen as if you were going to have to pass a test on how life is for the person speaking. You can certainly interject an open-ended question or two from the list of interview questions in Chapter 16. But this is strictly so you can learn more about their needs as they relate to your organization.

2. Connect

Once you have heard someone out, there is usually something obvious that needs to be said. Often it is merely to thank them for letting you know all of this and to acknowledge that you have, in fact, been listening. It may be a sincere thank you that they were willing to be so honest with you. "Though it's never pleasant to hear, we need that kind of feedback."

If they were expressing a concern or complaint, often an apology is needed at this point in the conversation. Even if it doesn't seem like an apology is called for, it can be a good place to start. While it may seem disingenuous to apologize for the organization's mistake 10 years ago, you can certainly tell someone you are sorry they have been so upset about the incident, or you are sorry it caused them to reduce their participation with your group.

Sometimes the way to connect is through humor. If the situation they are recounting was badly handled, you may need to poke fun at yourself, to humble yourself and your organization in some way. A confession can be helpful at this point as well. "I am terribly embarrassed this happened to you." "We really blew it with you, didn't we?" Telling a personal story or sharing something personal is also a good way to connect. "Something like that happened to me once, and I never wanted to go back to that company." "I have children too, and I know how frustrating that can be."

In most "botched" customer-service situations, some type of corrective action is the most effective way to connect. And there usually is a "fix," some way to repair the damage done. If you have listened closely to the person's concerns and authentically connected with them, they will trust you enough to let you suggest a fix. By now, it should have become clear what they would need to feel better. If not, you may need to ask: "How can we ever make this up to you?" "Is there any way we can win you back?" "What can we do to prevent this from ever happening again?"

But you have got to mean it. Whatever solution you arrive at, be sure you can deliver when you promise to take action. This time, the situation must be handled to perfection. You need to dazzle them with the sensitivity and efficiency of your organization, even if it means handling every detail of the solution yourself.

A commitment to winning back unhappy customers always pays off, and in the nonprofit world, it pays off in more dollars contributed. Unhappy customers don't want to be unhappy. They want to be heard. They want you to empathize with their plight. Then they want you to get a bandage, fix it, and make it better. They want to come back and be happy customers. They want to live happily ever after with you. It justifies their decision to get involved with you in the first place. It reinforces that they made the right choice.

At this point, you have connected. You are being authentic with them; you are being a real person, not a robot. This is essential to building a bridge to the next point on the Cultivation Superhighway: appreciation and acknowledgment. If you have ever tried to compliment someone who is upset or angry, you know they cannot hear it. It seems like sickening sugar-coating rather than the genuine acknowledgment you mean it to be. You cannot acknowledge someone until you have heard them out, until you have let them unload their stories and complaints, until you have connected with them enough that they trust you and can actually hear what you have to say.

3. *Appreciate and Acknowledge*

After you have listened, connected, and promised to take whatever action is needed, you must acknowledge the person and express your appreciation of them. Appreciation and acknowledgment are critical to success on the superhighway. If properly timed and delivered sincerely and authentically, true appreciation and acknowledgment can open up the channels of contribution unlike anything else.

By now you should know what the person would most want to be acknowledged for and how you, a person in your position in the organization, could appropriately acknowledge them for that. Tell them what you appreciate about them or about the interaction you have just had. "Having this conversation has reminded me how much I appreciate your insights and perspective on our work. You are a true friend of this organization (or this cause)." "We don't tell you enough how much it means to have someone like you involved with our organization." "No one else plays the role you do."

As a culture, we are stingy about doling out praise and appreciation, yet we love to receive it. It is better to err on the side of over-acknowledging someone rather than presuming only a bit will do.

Especially in the case of people you do not particularly like or enjoy, it may be difficult to find something genuine to say to acknowledge and appreciate the person. Here are some suggested opening phrases for those more challenging situations:

- "I know I can always count on you to (represent our constituents, speak your mind, tell me where we need to improve, etc.)."
- "I know you are passionate about (the needs of the people we serve, the basic values that we stand for, the future growth of our organization)."
- "I know I can trust you to (let me know when we're off base, 'read the pulse' of our community and let me know how we're doing)."

Regardless of whether the person is difficult or easy for you to praise, here are some tips to insure your heart-felt acknowledgment is well-received:

As much as possible, put yourself in the other person's shoes and imagine what they would want to be acknowledged for. The more relevant the acknowledgment to their particular situation, the better.

Think about how you can honestly express your appreciation to them. Right now, in spite of the fact that the situation is not fully resolved, what could you acknowledge this person for? Perhaps you could acknowledge them for their commitment to the mission of the organization, for their willingness not to stop until this is resolved, for helping you craft a solution to prevent this problem from happening again. What could you honestly say that would not sound artificial or contrived?

If you are not the best person to deliver this acknowledgment, who is? Whose words of appreciation would make the greatest impact? Given your role in the organization, you may not be the ideal person and yet there you are, in the car, on the phone, in the elevator with this person. You have just heard their story, connected person-to-person. You have offered to convey their concerns to the proper person. Perhaps you have offered to arrange a meeting of all the key people involved to let everyone air their thoughts.

Do not be concerned if you are not the best person. Ideally, you will be able to arrange for the executive director or the board chair or whomever that perfect person is, to deliver the kind words. In the interim, however, you may be the best there is. Think about what you could say. What could a person in your position say as an interim acknowledgment that would not sound too syrupy or insignificant? Is it also something you should put in a letter, and should you send a copy to the person's boss or their personnel file?

Assuming you are the "right" person, be generous with your appreciation. Lay it on as thick as you can while still being authentic. A good test of your authenticity is noticing yourself becoming moved just delivering the acknowledgment.

Be as specific as possible. Let the person know what actions or qualities about them you have noticed. Give some evidence of their greatness. Often, what people most want to hear are the acknowledgments for the little things they do time after time, the mundane things that go unrecognized.

In the Raising More Money workshops, we have people write a one or two-page acknowledgment letter to themselves, just to get a feel for what people want to hear. Usually, they whine and complain when they first hear this assignment. Once they start writing, they don't want to stop. They recognize that we can never hear enough of the good things. They come to realize that the little sappy lines make a difference.

Timing is key. You can safely assume you are already too late with your acknowledgment. At the pace of life today, we have become accustomed to instantaneous response and feedback. The days of sending the pretty thank-you note two weeks after the fact are over. People can barely remember what they did two weeks ago, let alone take the time to sit down and read your heartfelt letter. That is not to say you shouldn't write the thank-you letter anyway. Just do it the *same* day, or better yet call or email, and then follow up with a letter. Use the kind of words the other person will understand. Talk to them the way you would normally talk to them; keep the tone natural and conversational, not too formal or informal.

Consider ending your acknowledgment with a question or invitation so that the ball is in their court. For example, "If there is any other feedback you feel we should know as we begin to plan next year's event, I hope you will give me a call in the next week or two."

The Zone

Those of us who live in Seattle (though it is now available around the country), have become spoiled by the Nordstrom approach to customer service. I have come to expect that every time I walk into the store, someone will compliment me for something: how nice my hair looks, how much they like my scarf, etc. Even though I know this is part of their customer cultivation system, it works! Within one minute of walking into the store, I feel like a better, more attractive person. It alters my mood. I am suddenly checking myself out in the nearby mirror and noticing I do look pretty nice today. Maybe I ought to treat myself to a little something in the store.

That feeling is where you are going with all your appreciation and acknowledgment, to the final step on the Cultivation Superhighway called the Zone. The Zone is a land of its own, a land like no other, a land where there are no formal rules, a land where new things can happen. The Zone is where contribution is freely flowing. When you have arrived at the Zone, you won't need to ask people to give. They will know what to do. Your job will be to get out of their way and facilitate the gift they want to make. In the Zone, people want to give.

The Ongoing Cultivation Process

Once people have been to a Point of Entry event, received a personal Follow-Up Call where they are asked for their honest feedback, and asked how they might like to become involved, you begin to figure out how you can give them what they want. You find legitimate reasons for keeping in touch with them, several times a year. You may notice they begin calling you with thoughts or ideas they have to share. They may have read something or heard something that relates to your organization's work. Perhaps they discovered a colleague or acquaintance who has something to offer. Your organization is on their minds. They are out there, in the informal world of connections and conversations, talking and thinking about your organization.

This is the cultivation process—ever deepening their interest and involvement, always listening to their concerns and creatively delivering on what they are asking for, customized to their unique circumstances. Along the way, if they are honest with you, they will have questions and concerns. Perhaps their friends have raised questions or objections about your programs. They may need more information to respond to those objections; they may want you to meet with their friends directly. Each situation will be different.

Get in the habit of zipping though the first steps of the superhighway in every one-on-one interaction you have. It doesn't have to take more than a minute or two. Hear them out, reconnect authentically, person to person, then genuinely appreciate and acknowledge them for their commitment to your organization in whatever specific way is called for at that moment.

Then you are back to the Zone, the land where you can create something new, where you can meet together with their friend and see a whole new way to fund that project they have been wanting to make happen for you—smoothly and effort-lessly. This is fund raising at its best, where the giving of money is a natural part of the never-ending cultivation cycle. It is fund raising with no big artificial Asks, just a naturally generous offer to make a true contribution on the part of a faithful supporter who has been listened to, appreciated and is ready to give again.

At the same time, this does not mean that people will neces-sarily wake up in the morning and, with no other prompting, think, "Oh, this is the day I think I'll give a large gift to my favorite organization." They need a nudge. They need a re-minder—a call from you, a note, perhaps a meeting with their accountant to remind them that now would be a good time to begin giving.

The difference is that in this model your donors have been warmed-up to your organization at a pace they felt comfortable with. They know the facts, they have the emotional connection to your work, they have stayed connected to you in a way that works for them. They know that someone from your organiza-tion knows them. When they receive the nudge, it will be nothing more than nudging them toward something they were ready to do anyway. It will be nudging the inevitable.

CHAPTER 14

STEP THREE:
ASKING

In our model, the key to successful, terror-free asking, is the answer to only one question: Is this person *ready* to be asked? Another way of saying it is: Have we gotten to know this person enough so that it would feel natural to ask them to make a financial contribution to the organization now? Would asking this person now be nothing more than nudging the inevitable?

If your answer is anything other than a resounding YES, if it feels to you as if it is too soon to ask, then wait. Go back, re-listen, re-involve, re-cultivate, until the person is sufficiently engaged.

In our model, if you are starting with someone brand new to your organization and you have followed the process as described, it should take no more than six to nine months before the person is ready to be asked.

Keep thinking about picking fruit. A day or a week too early and you will have wasted all that time you spent growing and cultivating. Pace yourself to the donor. Some ripen faster than others. After you have trained yourself to notice the cues, you will feel more confident. Some examples of common cues from donors are: a prior in-kind gift, some other type of volunteer involvement, inviting other friends to become involved in your organization, or attending mission-oriented events.

The Fear of Asking

Most of the fear associated with asking for money has nothing to do with money. It is our fear of asking for *anything*. There you are at the fancy dinner party, sitting at the round table of 10 people, desperately scheming how to have the salt or butter passed to you from the other side of the table. Asking seems like intruding. It seems rude. It seems selfish. From a very young age, we have been taught not to intrude.

Stop for a minute and think about the breakthrough you said you wanted to produce for your organization, the legacy you want to leave. How badly do you want that? How big a difference would it make to your organization to have that? Now think about how good it feels to contribute to something you believe in, to contribute whatever you have in abundance—your time, talent or money, your old computers, your old pots and pans, that stock you bought at a very low price.

The main reason people say they hate asking for money is because they fear they will get a "No." It is worth pausing here to take a lesson from a nagging kid. Have you ever tried to tell one of them no? Notice how, before you know it, they are back in your face asking for it again, this time in a different way. "Okay, so you won't take me to the store now, how about later? When will you take me? Weren't you saying you needed some things at the store today?"

Kids are master askers. When they want something badly enough, they won't stop asking until they get it. They are creative and playful about it; to them it is a game. They deal with it like sparring. They throw you a punch, you throw one back. It tells them where to block and where to throw the next punch. It is just a big game or contest to them.

That is the zone you are aiming for when you are in the asking dance—playful, listening, friendly give-and-take, always with a dead-serious commitment to the result. And the more fun you can have with the process, the better. Laugh, poke fun at yourself—or maybe even at them if it is appropriate to the situation. Keep it as light as possible. If you can play with Asking that way, like two little puppies sparring in the yard, you will have much more fun and much more success.

People Prefer Saying Yes

Think of the last time someone asked you for something and you said no. How did it make you feel? Most people feel like they are being mean when they say no. We feel like a much nicer person when we say yes. People prefer saying yes.

When I ask people to contribute money to an organization, I always assume they would prefer to say yes. In fact, I assume they are looking for a way to say yes to precisely what I am asking for. We may just need a little give-and-take to work out the details. Details like: At what level would they feel most comfortable giving? Would they like to make their gift in honor or in memory of someone? Over how many years would they like to make their gift?

Your main job as the asker is to keep the donor in the driver's seat at all times. After all, it is their abundant resources they are being generous enough to contribute. The donors are the people doing the giving. You are the organization doing the receiving.

The only way you will ever get a no is if you ask. The good news is: if you never ask anyone for anything, odds are, you will never hear a no. The bad news is, you will never hear a yes either. The road to yes is paved with plenty of no's.

What Else Can No Mean?

Think back to the last time you said no to someone's request. What were you really saying? Most likely, it was not a flat, unequivocal no. Did you mean "Not now, ask me later?" or "Not that. Ask me for something else?" Or perhaps you meant "Not quite that. You're close, but you haven't hit on it exactly." In many cases, the word no does not mean a flat-out no.

If you are a person who will be asking for money for your favorite organization, from time to time you will hear no. Consider it a sign that you are on the right track. Welcome those no's! They are like gems. They tell you everything you need to re-frame your next Ask. Without them, you are shooting in the dark. You would not have a clue what the person is really thinking.

My general rule of thumb is to be prepared for the person to say no three times before they say yes. Remember, without the no's, you will never get to yes.

Leveraging Each Ask

By now it should be clear that if you want the gift, you are eventually going to have to ask for it. Even if people are ready to give, if the fruit is ripe and hanging from a low branch, someone needs to pick it.

Sure, people may send you a small check in response to a seasonal mailing, for example. If you rely on those appeals only, you will accustom your donors to giving smaller amounts several times a year. They will feel that they have given, albeit at only a fraction of their potential. The donor doesn't know what you need and what you will be happy with.

In order to fully leverage each Ask, our model requires asking each donor to make a Multiple-Year Pledge for unrestricted operating support by giving at one of our pre-set levels or Units of Service. Ideally, to leverage each gift further, a Challenge Gift is also offered. The final thing to consider in leveraging each Ask is the venue: Where will the Ask take place?

By walking into each asking situation having thought through these variables as they apply to that particular donor, you will feel much more prepared for a yes.

Preparing for Each Ask

The way to prepare yourself for an Ask is to do just that, *prepare*. People are often surprised by how much thought and preparation goes into each Ask—even after you have done the cultivation work.

I recommend you answer these questions for each and every personal Ask you make:

1. Exactly who will be asked? Have you been cultivating all the key decision-makers? Should spouses, partners, children, parents, or business partners be included? Including them in the Asking meeting or call tells them you respect their "vote" in the process. Down the road, they may be your main donor.

2. Who will do the asking? One person or more than one? Are these the people most appropriate to be asking this particular donor? Would another board member enhance the asking team? Is the asker too closely connected to the donor? Would a slightly more distant asker be better? Who is this donor's favorite person at the organization? Looking from the donor's self-interest, by whom would they be most flattered to be asked? To whom could this person not say no?

3. Where will the Ask take place? Ideally, would it be your place or theirs, at a restaurant or an office? Are you prepared for it to happen spontaneously at another location that may be more convenient for the donor?

4. Exactly what will be asked for? It is fine if the Ask includes more than one component: to make a leadership gift to the Sponsor-an-Artist Fund, as well as to co-chair the annual event or be a regional campaign chair. It tells the person you are looking for a longer-term relationship. You value them for their many talents and resources, not just their money.

5. What is the bottom-line gift you are after? It is good to have a range of Asks, starting with the biggest, then scaling

back to the bottom-line. It is often helpful to include items other than money in what you are asking for.

6. What makes you think this person is ready to be asked now? Have there been any recent cues? Have you hinted to the donor that you will be asking for their support soon? Keep putting yourself in the donor's shoes. Will they feel comfortable and receptive to an Ask now?

7. What are your biggest concerns, fears and reasons for procrastinating in making this Ask? Often these are legitimate, especially if they concern donor-readiness.

8. Does the person have an abundance of what you are asking for? Remember, they want to say yes. Don't embarrass them by asking for something which, from their perspective, they barely have enough of. You may need to do more homework to find out.

9. What is the person's self-interest in saying yes? How good would they feel saying yes? How sorry will they feel saying no? Ultimately, their emotional connection to your mission is what will sustain them as a lifelong donor.

10. What might strengthen this Ask? What could you add to the Ask that would make it nearly impossible for the person to say no? A different asker? An additional asker? A memorial gift? A leadership gift? A challenge or matching gift? More years to spread out the payment? A particular type of recognition?

11. How would this person most like to be recognized? Donors will never bring up recognition. You must weave it into the Ask. Let them know how "all donors at this level" will be recognized—special receptions with the scholarship recipients, meetings with important speakers, dinners at elegant homes, and so on. Try to give them two or three options for recognition.

12. How can this person invite others to participate? Once they have said yes, their natural tendency will be to want to share

their enthusiasm for this organization with others. It is good to mention some of those opportunities during the Ask.

13. What would be possible for your organization if the person says yes? Spend some time thinking through your response to this question, not only what it would mean for your programs and services, but what it could mean for the donor. Perhaps she would like to be asked to join your board. Think about the donor's Treasure Map. Who else might they naturally want to involve or let you invite to a Point of Entry?

14. What other questions are still unanswered? If you have answered all of the above questions thoroughly, you have probably uncovered some new ones. Remember, the more armed you feel going into the Ask, the better.

Now, find someone to role play the Ask with you. Give them the background on the person to be asked. Tell them some of your biggest fears so they can be sure to play on them during the practice session.

Be Authentic

Once you have thoroughly done your preparation, you need to put it all aside. Go into the Ask with an entirely different agenda: to see how related and connected you can become in those few minutes you will be together. It is all about listening for every cue and being much more focused on what they are saying right now than on what you should say next.

The key to a successful Ask is you being a real human being—not a robot with a script but a regular person who truly cares about this organization and this donor. The more authentic you can be, the better.

Asking someone for money is an intimate occasion. It can be serious, playful, short and to the point or long and drawn-out. No two Asks are ever the same, because no two people are the same. I recommend you approach it more like your first dance with your new, lifelong dance partner. You may step on each others' toes, grumble and laugh a bit, but eventually you will get it right. As with dancing, one person is the leader. In asking for money, it should go without saying that the donor is the leader.

To summarize: in our model, everything flows much more smoothly if you only ask for money from potential donors when you already know they will want to contribute. Asking should be nothing more than nudging the inevitable.

You are asking people who already know and love your organization. You already know they have what you are asking for. You already know they are emotionally connected to you.

Even so, they may say no to some or all of what you ask for. Your job if they do say no is to thank them for being a friend of your organization and to ask if there are any other ways they would like to be involved. Then your job is to figure out how to ask them again in exactly the way they want to be asked for exactly the thing they do want to say yes to. And then you ask them again, or have the perfect person ask them, so they say yes and feel great about it.

If they say yes and don't feel great about it, it is not a "win." You don't want to leave them with that icky feeling, that sense of having been manipulated into giving more than they were comfortable giving. You don't need their contribution that badly. You want each donor to feel as though they have sprinkled fairy dust on the most worthy organization in the world. You want each donor to feel so good about giving to you that they have no need for others to even know they did it. You want them to feel as if supporting your organization is a source of personal pleasure for them.

You have to let them know how excited you are to receive their gift. You cannot be just a little bit appreciative. Let them know right away that their gift was a big deal to you. Then you will have made a real friend. You have allowed them to truly contribute and to feel the way you feel when you know you have made a real contribution.

CHAPTER 15

MAKING
THE MOST OF
EVERY ASK

As we said in the last chapter, using this model there are several ways to maximize the potential of each Ask. We will discuss each of them more fully here.

Multiple-Year Giving Society

By following the Raising More Money model, you will build a system of lifelong donors by launching a Multiple-Year Giving Society. This will become the new, higher order of giving for those who truly support your cause. Giving at one of these levels is the donor's way of saying, "Count me in. I really do understand what your organization is up to. You have my permission to come back to me, to keep me involved and to ask me for more." From the perspective of the organization, members of your Multiple-Year Giving Society become a distinct group to cultivate, involve, and encourage to introduce other potential donors.

Launching your Multiple-Year Giving Society in no way precludes single-year giving. If you have a strong base of year-to-year donors, you will of course want to invite them to become part of your new, multiple-year program. If they decline this invitation, their names will still be listed in your Annual Report using the same categories you have used in the past.

Once you have established your Multiple-Year Giving Society you will want to list its members prominently as a separate category in your Annual Report, right above your annual givers. Be sure to use a big headline that calls attention to the fact that these people have agreed to give at these levels for the number of years stated.

Organizations are often reluctant to launch a Multiple-Year Giving Society. They usually say something like: "Our donors would never go for that." In truth, they are usually looking at it from their perspective, which is to say they would feel uncomfortable asking for multiple-year pledges.

Remember, the multiple-year Ask is not for the organization; the multiple-year Ask is for the donor. Multiple-year donors are people who already love you and in many cases have been giving to you, year after year, with relatively little contact or cultivation. Now you are giving them an opportunity to come forward and declare themselves part of your organizational family. Some will say, "No thank you." Others will ask: "What took you so long to notice?"

I recommend starting your Multiple-Year Giving Society with pledges of five years. Those organizations bold enough to write those few extra words "for five years" on their pledge cards, almost always wish they had done it sooner. Sometimes with extremely reticent groups, I have let them off the hook by asking for a three-year pledge. Invariably they come back to report that after seeing how many people selected that option, they wish they had increased it to five years or more. Five years goes by pretty quickly in the life of a donor, three years even more so. For many established organizations, I recommend starting with a 10-year commitment.

Without the multiple-year Ask, you are back to a standard old-reality, annual gifts program which, if done well, leaves the donor quietly giving year after year. Multiple-year asking, if done consistently, will grow your base exponentially and build the lifelong donors you are looking for.

Units of Service

Your Units of Service are the giving levels within your Multiple-Year Giving Society. They are the various bite-sized amounts of unrestricted funding you will be asking for. You should aim to have a total of only three levels. Start your lowest level at $1,000 a year to sponsor a child or a student, for example. That is $83 a month. Remember, while many donors will think, "$1,000 a year? They have got to be kidding!" others will think, "I could easily do that. I spend $83 dollars a month on so many things that are less important to me. This one really matters. I'd love to do that!"

Your middle unit should be in the $10,000 to $15,000 a year range. Your highest unit should be at least $25,000 a year.

Some organizations choose to add a unit for endowment. I recommend starting that unit at $20,000, which can be pledged over four or five years. Twenty thousand dollars, when invested conservatively at 5%, yields $1,000 a year in interest. That $1,000 is precisely what it takes to fund the lowest level in your Multiple-Year Giving Society, such as sponsoring a child or a student. That endowment "unit" can then be referred to as "$20,000 to endow services to a child."

Your Units of Service or multiple-year giving levels should have names that relate to your programs or services. Your units also must relate logically to one another. This can be accomplished easily if you use the same variable in naming them. As with everything else in our model, they must personalize your work. For example, if your lowest level was to sponsor a child, your middle level could be to sponsor a family, and your highest level could be to sponsor a neighborhood or a community. A sports group might choose for its units: sponsor a player, a team, and a league.

If you do not have obvious categories, consider more generic names like friend, mentor, or advocate. For advocacy or social change groups we have used levels such as $1,000 to mobilize five advocates or one community outreach worker who in turn trains 200 families a year. The name of the category must be brief. Using this same example, the official name of the unit would be "mobilize five advocates." Then, next to it in smaller type, could be a statement such as "each advocate trains 200 families a year."

Take some time to come up with a strong overall name for your Multiple-Year Giving Society since it will be with your organization for years. Consider the name of a famous person who has been a champion for your cause. Or perhaps the name of one of your founders or founding board members. It is also fine to use a more generic category, like the more traditional Founder's Society, Legacy Club or the Friends of (your organization).

How to Design Your Units of Service

The main thing to keep in mind as you design your Units of Service is that you will be making it clear to your donors that these levels represent arbitrary chunks of needed, unrestricted operating funds. They will be giving at these levels because they believe in your overall mission. They trust you to get the job done. If they have questions about your use of funds, they can review your audit.

In other words, your units or levels do not have to be accurate to the penny. The easiest way to justify your Units of Service is to take your total budget or total budget shortfall and divide it by roughly the number of people you serve in a year. For example, let's assume the total budget for your organization is $2 million. After deducting your public funding and the fees you charge your art patrons or health-care patients, you arrive at a number of $200,000 you must raise privately each year. Since you are aiming for your lowest unit to be $1,000, what variable could you divide $200,000 by to arrive at $1,000? In other words, what do you serve or provide 200 of each year? Families, homeless women, acres of land being preserved, pregnant teenagers or dance patrons? That will give you your lowest unit. Then work up from there based on the variable you have chosen. It all needs to hang together and make logical sense to a donor.

Once you have designed your units, do not change them. On the contrary, try to universalize them within your system. Include these units in all your solicitations. The pledge card you design for your Multiple-Year Giving Society will be the same pledge card you use in all of your solicitations, including the Free One-Hour Asking Event. A sample pledge card can be found on page 209.

As you become comfortable with the levels you have designed, you will find it easy to make all of your Asks at one of these levels. I often tell the story about asking for a contribution from the owner of a large, privately-held corporation. This man had attended a Point of Entry event, had been well followed-up and cultivated. He was definitely ready to be asked. Because of his heavy travel schedule, I had been unable to connect with him by phone to even schedule a time we could get together to discuss his gift.

A month or so later, I happened to nearly bump into this man as he was coming out of an elevator in the lobby of an office building. Our 20-second conversation went something like this:

"Hi, Terry, how are you? I know I owe you a call."

"Yes, that's OK. You know why I was calling."

"Yep, I do. What's everybody giving?"

"$25,000 a year for 5 years to 'Sponsor a Classroom' of kids."

"That sounds great. Sign us up!"

If you have followed the model, not skipped over any of the steps, and have your Units of Service well thought out, an Ask can be that simple. So it is well worth taking the time to custom design the Units of Service that best suit your organization.

Challenge Gifts

One final leveraging tool which can make a major difference in your asking success is the Challenge Gift. Whether given by one donor or pooled by several donors into a Challenge Gift Fund, when used as a matching gift, it gives the donor the perception of a bargain. And we all love a bargain. Here is how it works.

First, go through your donor lists and rank your donors by giving potential. Then rank them again based on their passion for your cause. The handful who shake out at the top of *both* lists are your candidates for giving funds that can be used as part of the Challenge Gift.

Next, set your goal. Say you want to raise $100,000. Ask the top five donors from your lists if they would each consider giving you $10,000. Tell them you would like to use their collective $50,000 as a one-to-one match for gifts from other donors.

Then, at the usual time of year for your annual campaign, go to your other potential donors, the ones who are a bit farther down the lists. Tell them this year you have been presented with a wonderful opportunity: a group of your major donors has come together to stimulate the campaign to reach a new level. They have put $50,000 into a Challenge Gift Fund. Every dollar given will be matched one-to-one by this Challenge Fund. And there is a deadline by when you must fulfill the challenge.

For donors who work for a company that matches employee contributions, this can mean a four-to-one leverage of their gift. They give $1,000, their company matches it so it becomes $2,000, and your Challenge Gift Fund donors match that amount, so the total gift becomes $4,000. The value of leveraging their gift in this way will not be lost on most of these folks.

Be sure to clarify with your Challenge Fund donors—the ones who seed the initial $50,000 in this example—what kind of a challenge they want to offer. Will their money match other donations dollar for dollar, two for one or three for one? Also decide in advance how you want to handle donor pledges. Will they "count" in the match? Will those who pledge still give you the full amount of the their Challenge Gift even if you don't fulfill the match? Will the employer's matching portion of each gift count in the base gift to be matched by your Challenge Gift Fund?

Another highly effective twist: Use the Challenge Gift Fund to match only the increased portion of a donor's gift. In other words, if they gave $500 last year, the challenge funds may match whatever amount the donor gives beyond $500 this year.

Think through all the ways you can promote the Challenge Gift Fund. Decide if you want to showcase the founding donor or donors to the fund. How can they help you bring in more donors? Can you write about it in your newsletter, include it in other mailings, send out a special announcement about it, kick it off at the annual event?

Before you announce the Challenge Fund, put together several foolproof strategies for fulfilling on it. You will need 10 gifts of $5,000, 20 gifts of $1,000, etc. Be sure that you, personally, are excited about the potential of the Challenge Fund for your organization. What will it provide in the way of programs and services? Can you articulate this to potential donors?

People want to know that you need their support and that you will use it wisely. The more you can leverage their gift, the more of a "bargain" they feel they are getting for it, the better.

The Venue for the Ask

Having considered how to design your Units of Service within your Multiple-Year Giving Society and how to stimulate giving with a Challenge Gift, there is one more key variable to consider if you want to make the most of every Ask: the venue.

Where is this Ask going to take place? What medium will be used for asking? Will the Ask take place by letter, by phone, by email or in person? If it will be done in person, will it be done individually or at a larger group asking event such as the Free One-Hour Asking Event used in our model?

All of the evidence supports asking in person if you want to receive the largest gift possible. Knowing your donor or potential donor as well as you will at this point, put yourself in their shoes: how would they most prefer to be asked for that size gift?

Time permitting, individual in-person Asks should always be your first choice, but do not overlook the power of a group Ask at a single-purpose free asking event. If a critical mass (at least 20%) of your guests have been through a true Point of Entry and have been followed-up one by one, sometimes the group Ask can save time and produce a sense of community that will generate larger gifts that many people would give on their own. Plus, it allows you to control the script of the Ask, clarifying your Multiple-Year Giving Society and your Units of Service, insuring that people understand they are making an unrestricted gift.

Chapter 23 goes into much greater detail about how the Free One-Hour Asking Event works. I encourage you to consider it as a serious contender for a venue for a group Ask. For many organizations who are concerned about adopting this model with limited staff, this event can provide a relatively painless way to launch your Multiple-Year Giving Society in a mere 60 minutes.

CHAPTER 16

STEP FOUR:
MULTIPLE-YEAR DONORS
INTRODUCING OTHERS

We are now ready to talk about the last step in the model where our happy, Multiple-Year Giving Society donors talk about us with their friends and, ultimately, introduce their friends to the organization by inviting them to attend a Point of Entry event.

This is a natural occurrence for most people who have made a multiple-year gift. They feel good about their gift, and they will be happy to hear from you. It is also an opportunity to deepen your relationship with them. How? As always, you do this by asking them questions you would truly like the answers to and listening to their responses—and then inviting them to a Point of Re-Entry event.

As your donors become a part of your Multiple-Year Giving Society, their names are removed from any other solicitation programs such as direct mail or telemarketing. The type and frequency of all future contacts with them is determined by their Donor Services Representative or by the key development staff person.

The First Contact After the Gift

The first contact should be a telephone call within three days of their first multiple-year gift. The easiest way to do this is to speak to each donor by telephone shortly after they have joined the Multiple-Year Giving Society. You can follow the basic Follow-Up Call script: Thank you for your gift. Or thank you for coming to our fund-raising event. Or thank you for becoming a member of our Sponsor-a-Family Program.

Now that they are part of your family, you can go a little deeper. Tell them how much you value their support and their input. Ask them a few more questions: What is it about your organization that particularly interests them? Do they have any advice for you? Is there any other way they might like to become involved? Is there anyone else you should invite to a Point of Entry event?

It may be appropriate at this point to ask them to host a Point of Entry event—to invite a group to a special tour of your facility, or to host something at their home, office, religious organization, golf club—wherever would be easiest for their friends to gather. If you will be doing the Free One-Hour Asking Event, this may be the time to ask your new, happy multiple-year donors if they would consider being a Table Captain at the event which can then serve as a Point of Entry for their guests.

Another opportunity for donors to introduce others is to encourage them to bring a friend to your Free Feel-Good Cultivation Events (see Chapter 22). There they will be in the company of many happy donors, including their particular donor/friend, who are being reconnected to the mission of the organization at a Point of Re-Entry event. This will serve to accelerate their getting-acquainted process.

Since these new, happy, Multiple-Year Giving Society donors have attended a Point of Entry event, received your Follow-Up Calls, and were asked to give only after being sufficiently involved and inspired, they trust you will do the same with their friends. They are turning over to you their most precious gift, their friends and family. These are people who trust them, people with whom they have a reputation to preserve. You need to treat their friends with the utmost care and respect. In every interaction, you need to demonstrate your professionalism and tact in maintaining the confidentiality of the original donor. Do not make assumptions about their friendship with the person they have introduced you to.

The dream, of course, is that each of these newly-referred guests becomes a lifelong donor with an even larger and more-inspired commitment than the friend who initially referred them. If you take great care of them, personalizing your approach to each of them at the Point of Entry event and the follow up, you will see how quickly they lead you to more and more donors making multiple-year pledges for larger and larger amounts. You will see how our circle model quickly spirals upward exponentially.

Now that you understand the basics of the model, we will look at several other issues to be considered as you tailor this approach to the unique needs of your organization.

CHAPTER 17

DESIGNING A KNOW-THY-DONOR PROGRAM

One of the first questions I ask when I start working with an organization is the obvious: "How many active donors do you have?" They can often proudly tell me a very large number somewhere in the many thousands. Next question: "How many of those donors does someone here actually know?" This means someone has, at a minimum, talked to them in person or on the phone. Invariably, the answer to this question is not many.

From time to time, I am called by progressive, new-reality, direct-mail companies to ask if I will work with their clients. "We've maxed out what we can do for them with mail. They've got to get to know these donors and grow them into major do-nors." They are right.

Most organizations do not need new donors. They have plenty of existing donors. Rather than starting their system with a Point of Entry which is designed to introduce potential new donors to the organization, they need to start by getting to know their existing donors. I call it a Know-Thy-Donor Program. As with everything else in this model, with a systematic effort over time, it will bear much fruit.

Once again, think of yourself as one of those loyal donors to your favorite organization. You have been giving faithfully for years, sending in checks in response to mail or phone appeals annually, quarterly or monthly. Yet no one has ever called you to say thank you or to acknowledge your gift in person. It is a wonder you keep giving.

Stratify Your Donors by Gift Level

Start your Know-Thy-Donor Program by getting the real numbers about your organization. How many individual donors have given to you in the last two years? What is each donor's total gift for each of those years? You may be surprised to see how much those $25 a month checks add up to, all from one loyal donor.

Now, classify the donors you have. How many give you, annually:

- $1,000 and above?
- $500 - $999?
- $250 - $499?
- $100 - $249?

Don't be surprised to find some who give more than $10,000 a year without a personal contact from you.

What are they telling you with this gift? For whatever reason, they are believers in your work. They may have only a superficial understanding of the work of your organization, yet they give. Perhaps they had a family member with the disease you are working to eradicate. Maybe their mother or father received services from your organization many years ago.

If you are working to build a self-sustaining individual giving program that is based on one-to-one personal relationships, knowing more about each donor would be a great help. And there is only one way to find out: Ask them!

Once you've analyzed the stratification of your existing donors, choose the cutoff level for your first round of calls. Let's say you decide to call all donors who give $500 or more a year and that you have 100 of them.

A High Level Thankathon

Start your Know-Thy-Donor Program by enlisting the support of a small group of your best and most passionate people. They should also be people who like talking on the telephone. It may be a mixed group of board, staff and volunteers.

Before you give them the list of donors to be called and a recommended script, it is wise for the most senior development staff person or volunteer to make five or ten of these calls personally. That way you will get consistent feedback, all screened through the eyes and ears of the same phoner. Based on what you learn in the first ten calls, you can then design a broader telephone survey which can be used by your team of callers.

When you are ready to put together a group of board and staff to phone these current donors personally, you can call it a Thankathon.

How should you start the calls? Yes, with a gracious and humble thank you. The main purpose of the call is to thank and appreciate the donor for their loyal support (and their recent gift if your timing is right). If you accomplish nothing else on this call, be sure they know how much you appreciate them.

Here is a suggested outline for the call:

> Hello, Ms. _____. My name is _____. I'm on the board of _____.
>
> You've been a loyal supporter for several/many years and we're calling to thank you. (Pause for response.) We're doing a little survey to learn what we could be doing better. Would you have a few minutes now for me to ask for your thoughts and advice?

Interview

Then, slowly, ask three or four of the open-ended Treasure Map Interview questions listed here, noting the donor's answers along the way. The questions below are typical, but you should do your own work to come up with a list of questions that reflect what your organization wants to know.

1. What do you already know about our organization?
2. What images come to mind when you think of us?
3. How did you come to know about us or become involved with us?
4. What do you like about being a friend/supporter of our organization?
5. Where or how do you think we're really missing the boat?
6. What advice do you have for us?
7. What cues might we have missed from you?
8. How better could we be telling our story?
9. What could we be doing to involve more people?

Invite Them to a Point of Entry

Each call should end with an invitation to attend a Point of Entry or Point of Re-Entry event and to bring others if they would like. If they agree to attend, follow up with a confirmation card and a reconfirmation call the day before. Offer to provide transportation if necessary.

Your Thankathon calling team can do the phoning in a group one afternoon or evening. Or they can make their calls on their own from their home or workplace. (Be sure they turn in their notes.) Imagine, for example, a team of five callers with each caller reaching five people a week. If you debrief well, you will have enough feedback to customize the next phase of the program.

I have seen board members get so excited about this that they recommend a Donor Services Representative Program or buddy system for pairing a volunteer or staff member with each donor above a certain dollar amount for two years. Imagine being a donor who hears from someone at their favorite charity three or four times a year—including invitations to a variety of special Free Feel-Good Cultivation Events. When it is time for making their annual gift next year, they will be hard pressed to say no to a request for a larger gift. They may even feel connected enough to make a multiple-year pledge when asked, especially if it will be doubled by a matching gift Challenge Fund.

Remember, these are your cherished donors, those names on your mailing list who are sending in small and medium-sized gifts on a regular basis. Show them the respect and care you would show your greatest treasures. And then show them your stuff!

Know-Thy-Donor Program

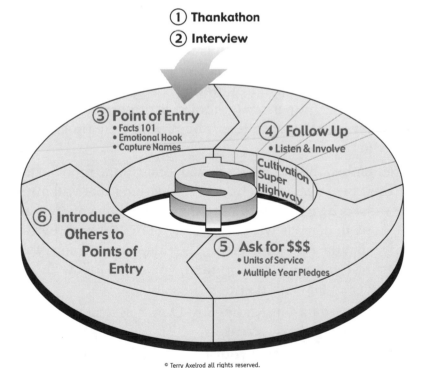

Follow Up; Keep them on the Cycle

Next, get these donors officially on your cycle. Dazzle them with your Point of Entry event: the Facts, the Emotional Hook, the needs, all the trimmings. Follow up within a week and get their feedback. How else might they like to become involved? Who else would they recommend you invite to a similar event? Then deliver on what they are requesting. Follow through impeccably with feedback on all their suggestions. Thank them for sending that friend to the next introductory event. Find lots of reasons to have more contact with them. Keep thinking of what else you might do to be responsive to their unique concerns.

Keep this system going. Have your phoning team keep calling and interviewing more prior donors from your data base, moving down to the $100 to $499 donors, and so on. Keep inviting donors to Point of Entry events. Keep re-educating, re-inspiring, and thanking them, the more personally the better.

One caution: You will come across donors who have been giving in response to mail and telephone solicitations who do not want more personal contact with you. They prefer an arms-length relationship. One option is to offer to have a one-on-one Point of Entry event for them. You can send them a copy of your video and follow up by phone a week later. Or you can keep them on your personal phoning list to update them as often as they would like to hear about your new programs and your needs.

Remember, this is a personalized, one-to-one model. People have their own distinct preferences. The thing that will impress them most is if you listen to how they are telling you they want to be kept in contact with and then follow through by doing exactly what they ask. Conversely, the thing that will annoy them most is if, after asking their opinion, you don't follow their advice when dealing with them.

Stay focused on this Know-Thy-Donor System and you will see your contributions increase.

You will be cultivating your base of lifelong donors.

DESIGNING YOUR RECOGNITION AND CULTIVATION SYSTEM

Recognition and cultivation go hand-in-hand. Most donors will tell you they are not looking for recognition. They get all the satisfaction they need just by giving to your organization. That may be only partially true.

Take a moment to think of yourself. Think of times you have been a donor, a board member, a volunteer, or a staff member. Think of the times you have been recognized in any of these roles. What did the organization say or do to recognize you? Did it work? Did it get the job done? How did it feel to you?

You may be surprised and embarrassed by how petty your responses seem. This is when the little things matter. Although the group may have tried their very best to genuinely recognize and appreciate you, they may have missed the mark.

When it comes to personal recognition, what matters most? When we take the time to do this exercise in some depth in the workshops, here are some of the things people say. "To be effective, the recognition needs to make me feel special and feel appreciated." " I need to know that they noticed or perhaps that a particular person (the boss, perhaps) noticed." "I need to feel that whatever I did really made a difference for the organization."

In other words, even though most donors will never bring up the topic of recognition, you should assume they want it. Although they may not want to have a big fuss made over them, at a minimum, unless they absolutely insist on remaining anonymous, they want someone to recognize that they do care and are a true supporter.

Rather than trying to second guess your donors and then provide them random appreciation and sporadic contacts, your organization is probably long overdue for a well-thought-out system of recognition and cultivation. Also, as your base of donors, volunteers, and friends grows, it will be helpful to have a system for tracking when and how you formally contact them to deepen the cultivation process.

Recognition is a key component in your system of personalized cultivation. As with many other aspects of the Raising More Money model, you are probably already doing a great deal to stay connected and say thank you. Yet without a recognition system that will live on beyond your tenure with your organization, your legacy will be incomplete and you will undermine your efforts to keep your donors for life.

Designing your recognition/cultivation system is relatively simple and can be fun. You will finally be able to give yourself credit for all the things you are doing right. The critical element in streamlining this process is to have all the key players in the room as you do it.

Identify Your Team

Start by identifying all the internal people who already have some part in the process. People whose work connects you to your broader community—the data entry person, the people who plan your special events, the grant writers, the development committee, the staff who work with donors and volunteers, the folks in the accounting department, and the board members.

Create a Recognition and Cultivation Matrix

Assemble all these folks, or at least one representative from each group, in one room where you have papered the walls with newsprint. Across the top, make 12 columns for the months of the year. Down the left side, list all your constituent groups, broken down as specifically as possible—donors at various levels, volunteers in various programs, clients or patrons in whatever categories you normally speak of.

Be sure to solicit the input from each member of the team. Each of you is an expert in one particular piece of the puzzle. Then go back and fill in the boxes, month by month, with what you are already doing to recognize or connect with those people in that month.

For example, if you normally have a volunteer recognition dinner for volunteers of a particular program in May, put the name of that event in the proper box. Regular mailings, newsletters, and annual reports can be added into the appropriate months. Other special events throughout the year should be inserted in the box for the group they are targeted for. You may want to color code all the mailings in yellow, all the events in blue, all the times donors will be asked for money in green, etc.

Clarify Who Is Accountable

Now go back and put the *title* (not the person's name) of the job description of the person accountable for making each of those things happen. If the personal hand-written holiday note to all donors over $5,000 is always written by the executive director, write that title in. If the invitation to the graduation ceremony is done by the Parents' Committee chairperson, write that title in.

Fill in everything you can think of. Then identify who else might be missing. You may realize that one of the satellite pro-

Sample Annual Recognition/Cultivation Plan

Legend: In Person · Mail · Fax · Phone · Online

	JANUARY	FEBRUARY	MARCH	APRIL	MAY	JUNE	JULY	AUGUST	SEPTEMBER	OCTOBER	NOVEMBER	DECEMBER
DONORS:												
Legacy Club (Endowment)	1 on 1 Luncheons with Executive Director and Board Chair				Private Dinner					Legacy Club Private Home Dinner		Asked to be Table Captains Next Year
Classroom Sponsors ($25,000/yr x 5 years)	1 on 1 Follow Up with Their Requests			Spring Field Day		Pre-Graduation Reception		Board-Hosted Golf Day with Lunch			Telephone Follow-up & Interviews	
Student Sponsors ($1,000/yr x 5 years)	Thank You Calls from Executive Director and/or Board Chair	Post-holiday Thankathon & Interviews; Invite to	Annual Report Mailed; Donor-Hosted Points of Entry or Re-Entry									Holiday Mailing to Non-Event Donors
$500 - $999												
$250 - $499												
$100 - $249												
<$100												
	← Newsletter →			Email and Fax Updates Monthly (All Year)					Invite to Free-one Hour Asking Event	← Newsletter →	Free-One Hour Asking Event	
VOLUNTEERS												
Current Board	Board Planning Retreat	Board/E.D. 1 on 1 Interviews					Email and Fax Updates Monthly (All Year)	Nominating Committee Re-up Calls				Board Recognition Dinner
Past Board												
Current Committee Members			Thank You Calls from E.D.	1 on 1 Meetings with E.D.								
Tutors	Site Visit from E.D.			Site Visit from E.D.			E.D. Site Visits			E.D. Site Visit		
Mentors				Mentoring Program Dinner	Volunteer Recognition Luncheon	Graduation (Reserved Seats)	Special Summer Program	Summer Graduation				
Computer Program Volunteers		Winter Concert	Computer Night									
Music Program Volunteers									Back-to-School Open House / Curriculum Fair			
	← Newsletter →	1 to 1 Notes and Birthday Cards from Supervisor (All Staff, All Year)										
STAFF												
Main Office		Administrative Staff Retreat										All Staff Holiday Party / Holiday Gifts to Staff
Program Staff			Program Staff Retreat		Staff Picnic							
Satellite Youth Program Staff				1 to 1 Notes and Birthday Cards from Supervisor (All Staff) [All Year]								

grams puts on some special educational evenings that you haven't been tracking. Better call that person and have them look over your matrix to give their input.

Next, as a team, stand back from the matrix and notice where there are empty boxes. Has a donor at the $500 to $1000 level not had contact from you for four months in a row? What would be a legitimate contact you could add in just the right month? Perhaps it would be a thank you call from the Thankathon Committee member or from their personal Donor Services Representative.

Then go back through the matrix, looking at the categories of people you have listed down the left-hand side. Take them one at a time and walk through the flow of the year from the perspective of those in that category. Does it make sense that they are receiving invitations and letters from three different people in the same month? Have you removed them from the direct-mail program once they begin giving at a certain level? Where in the annual cycle is the opportunity for each group listed to give feedback about how you are doing? Is there enough real-person contact or is too much via the mail? What other information are you missing? Flesh out your chart with the kind of rich detail you want future generations to know about.

Zoom in on the Donors

Now go back and zoom in on the donors. Make a separate, more detailed chart just for your donors. You may want to break down your donor categories even further for this. List them down the left-hand column by whatever names or categories you have established. Start with donors who give less than $100, next $100 to $500, then $500 to $1000. Make special categories for donors in your Multiple-Year Giving Society at each of the levels you offer there, even if you have not started one yet.

Next, across the top of the paper or white board, instead of writing the months of the year, you will be determining your own time categories. Each one will relate to the number of days since that donor's last gift. In other words, if your first column is

SAMPLE DONOR RECOGNITION/CULTIVATION PLAN

Legend: ☺ In Person ☒ Mail ☏ Phone 🖱 Online 📠 Fax

	Within 3 Days:	Within 1 Week:	2 Weeks Later	One Month Later	3 Months Later	6 Months Later	9 Months Later	One Year Later
LEGACY CLUB (ENDOWMENT)	Personal Thank You/ Interview Calls from E.D.	Invite to Next Legacy Club Event		1 on 1 Lunch with ED and Board Chair	Special Legacy Club Event: Outline the Next Vision and Follow Up	1 on 1 Call/Interview from E.D.: Next Steps?		Asked to Host Small Lunch or Dinner Point of Entry for Friends
CLASSROOM SPONSORS ($25,000/yr x 5 years)		Personal Thank You Call from Board Chair	Thank You Card from Classroom Signed by Kids (With Pictures)	Classroom Tour and Lunch; Follow Up Calls	Free Feel-Good Cultivation Event and Follow Up	Asked to Host Table at Free Asking Event	Asked to Host Special Point of Entry for Friends; then Follow-Up	Call with Pledge Reminder; Asked to Consider Challenge Gift
STUDENT SPONSORS ($1,000/yr x 5 years)	Personal Thank You/ Interview Call From D.D. [Selected Calls from E.D.]	Written Thank You Letter Signed by Board Chair	Thank You Card from Student with Artwork; Call from Donor Services Representative			Asked to Host One Hour Asking Event	Special Free Feel-Good Event Focusing on Next Needs of Organization	Asked to Increase Pledge at Annual Free One-Hour Asking Event
$500 - $999	Invite to Next Free Feel-Good Cultivation Event & Next Public Point of Entry		Follow up from D.D.: "What Else do you Need?" →Implement			2nd Follow Up Call from D.D.		Personal Solicitation Call or Visit from Board Member or Donor Services Representative
$250 - $499		Personal Thank You from D.D.				Interview and Invite to Next Free Feel-Good Cultivation Event; Assign to Donor Service Representative		
$100 - $249		Personal Thank You from D.D.			Additional Solicitation: Ask to Increase Giving Level	Additional Solicitation: Ask to Increase Giving Level		Additional Solicitation and Asked to Increase Gift at Free Event
<$100		Thank You Card With Personal Note from Student or Teacher						

Spanning arrows:
- Asked to be Table Captain Next Year →
- ← Formal IRS Thank You Letter →
- free Feel-Good Cultivation Event #1 and Follow Up
- free Feel-Good Cultivation Event #2 and Follow Up

labeled "within three days," you would fill in the box for each level of donor, stating what type of contact they would receive from your organization within three days of making their gift. I recommend that for any gift of $100 or more, you write in, "Personal thank you call from development staff or board member."

Now, moving across the top row, think about how frequently that donor would need to hear from you in order to stay connected. How many contacts would you want them to have before they are asked to give again? Here are some suggested categories to write across the top:

- Within three days after the gift is received
- Within one week
- Two weeks later
- One month later
- Three months later
- Six months later
- Nine months later
- One year later

These will be the trigger points for your regularly-scheduled contacts with each donor. Of course, these do not preclude additional contact. Let's say, for example, that in the "one month later" box, you always do a personal telephone interview, or perhaps you send out a written note if you can't reach the person after three attempts. If, in the personal interview, your donors tell you about another way they would like to become involved or request special information about one of your programs, you would need more frequent and timely contact to respond to those requests.

Put yourself in your donors' shoes as you fill in each box in this matrix. What kind of contact would they like six months later? Vary your media. Switch from phone to mail to online with some donors. If the donor has told you they prefer less frequent contact, how much less frequent?

At what point will you want to invite them to a Free Feel-Good Cultivation Event? How soon after that will they receive a Follow-Up Call? What other forms of personal recognition will you add? An invitation to lunch with a board member and the executive director? A special invitation to a dinner at a board member's home. You get the idea. The more customized you can make your chart, the better.

If you want to get elaborate, you can do this as a branching chart, the kind the computer folks use. If A, then B. If not A, then C, and so on.

The point is, paradoxically, to get you thinking generically about your customized donor recognition/cultivation system. While no two donors may ever follow precisely the same path, there is a certain generic checklist with trigger points along the way that you will want to use as a template.

Just as you did with your first chart, you will want to identify who is accountable for making sure each of these contacts happens. If you have designated fund development staff or Donor Service Representative, ultimately that will be the person. Yet, you will want to include many others in the process—board members, key volunteers, program staff, family members.

The easiest way to avoid becoming overwhelmed with the complexities of the process is to simply list out the time categories suggested above (three months later, six months later, etc.) and fill in the boxes for your typical donor. Then you can customize from there.

Regular Review

For both your recognition and your cultivation systems, be sure to designate someone who is accountable for bringing the team back together at least once a year (more often for the donor-only chart). This will be an opportunity for everyone to assess how the system is working and further refine the process.

CHAPTER 19

THREE TYPES OF EVENTS THAT GROW DONORS

Special events have become a way of life for most nonprofit organizations. Often, even when the events are intended to be fund raisers, the people in charge of putting them on cannot recall how much money the events are supposed to raise.

We all know the litany of complaints about the work and anxiety associated with events that don't seem to be building much of anything for the future. They are rarely designed with a follow-up system in mind.

In our model for Building a Self-Sustaining Individual Giving Program, any event your organization is now putting on can easily be recast to fit into one of the following three categories:

- Point of Entry Events
- Free Feel-Good Cultivation Events (also known as Points of Re-Entry)
- Free One-Hour Asking Events

The intention of this section on events is for you to be able to categorize and redesign, if necessary, each of your events, so they fit together in a strategic system that grows and strengthens your base of lifelong individual donors. Be forewarned: over time, this approach is likely to put an end to the one-year-at-a-time, "fund-raising fluff" special events.

Your Current Events

Start by making a list of all the events your organization currently puts on in a year. Include all types of events: annual dinners, holiday parties, volunteer and donor recognition events, anniversary events, golf tournaments, walk-a-thons, theater events, black tie galas, auctions. You can even include volunteer recruitment events, training classes, or actual performances of your arts organization.

Now let's define the three types of events used in this model:

1. Point of Entry event

By now, you are familiar with the three essential ingredients of a Point of Entry event: Facts, Emotional Hook, and being able to Capture the Names of the guests. Most of the events you have been calling "fund raisers" could easily be modified to become Points of Entry. It is fine to charge people money to come to a Point of Entry event. Just be sure that all of the objectives of a Point of Entry event have been accomplished before they leave.

Here is a little test of whether your event qualifies as a Point of Entry for your guests. The next day, if someone had asked them about the dinner-dance the night before or the golf tournament, could the guests have answered the following two-question pop quiz:

1. What was the name of the organization for which the event was raising funds?
2. What does that organization do?

What people will remember most is a video and a short testimonial from someone who has benefited from your work.

Do you have good records of the names and phone numbers of the guests? Moreover, would you have a legitimate reason for calling them after the event to find out what they thought of it? Or would that seem too contrived? What could you add to the event that would let those guests who might want more information identify themselves so you would have sufficient permission to follow up with them?

2. Free Feel-Good Cultivation Events (also known as Points of Re-Entry)

The name pretty much says it all. These are the "reward" events for your Multiple-Year Giving Society donors that re-connect them to the Emotional Hook and reinforce the wisdom of their investment in you. That means they always include a program or theme that ties to your mission.

Do not underestimate the magic of a "free" event. Regardless of people's capacity to pay for the event, when it comes time to ask them for the next contribution, if you re-inspired them, they will remember you gave them something for free. Just make sure you have one or more underwriters who receive plenty of credit, so your loyal donors will know you did not spend any of their money to pay for this.

To keep it simple, you can invite donors to internal events already planned to honor your clients or families such as graduations, show-and-tell nights, special theater performances or expert lectures.

Free Feel-Good Cultivation Events can be varied for donors at different giving levels. You may invite your biggest donors to an elegant dinner at the most exclusive private home or the home of a revered person in your field, if that is the sort of thing they would like. Your smaller Multiple-Year Donors might be invited to a dinner or lecture series, a family picnic or a special "environmental" day.

Just as with a Point of Entry event, a Point of Re-Entry always engenders a Follow-Up Call, eliciting more feedback, which in turn enables you to further customize your approach to each donor. This keeps the donor going around the cycle with you.

3. *Free One-Hour Asking Events*

Most organizations are not yet doing the type of event we are referring to here. To qualify as a Free One-Hour Asking Event in this model, the guests are invited verbally by a friend who serves as a Table Captain, to a free breakfast or lunch event.

The guests know in advance that they will be asked to give money at the event. The Table Captain also must be sure to inform them at the point of the invitation that there is "no minimum and no maximum gift" expected. As much as anything, you are asking them to come and learn more about the organization. It will be your job to inspire and educate them so they will want to give.

Asking events are ideally suited to the new reality because they are a straightforward, time-limited infomercial about the outstanding work of your organization. In one tightly-choreographed hour, they provide the Facts, the Emotional Hook and a compelling Ask for multiple-year support at specific giving levels.

This event is an extremely effective money raiser for the following reasons:

1. The majority of guests have already attended a "real" Point of Entry event and have been followed-up personally and involved. They serve as a critical mass within the larger group and provide a momentum towards giving.

2. The guests have been well prepared in advance and know giving will be optional at the event. You must base your financial projections on the assumption that only half of the guests will give at all. Then you will be pleasantly surprised.

3. The event is free. To repeat: In fund raising, "free" is magical. If you were to charge even $10 a person to attend this event, it would never be as successful. People are given a nice, basic breakfast or lunch, for which they do not feel

overly obligated. They are free to enjoy themselves and to give freely when asked, if they so choose. Do not do this event as a dinner. Dinner implies a greater degree of obligation which could get in the way of donors choosing freely how much they would like to give.

Some Soul-Searching Questions About Your Special Events

Before we look at retooling your existing events, let's put each event through some careful scrutiny. Without your staff, board, or event committee at your side, take the time now, while you are alone, to answer these questions honestly for each of the events your organization currently produces:

1. What have you said to justify not reaching your dollar goal for this event? Do any of the following statements sound familiar?

   "At least we made the board and volunteers happy."

   "We had no other choice; everyone expects us to put on this event; it's an annual tradition."

   "It's an opportunity to get our name out there in the community."

   "It lets us tell our story to a broader group of people."

   "It's a 'friend' raiser."

   Most of the time, these kinds of statements justify the fact that, in spite of your best efforts, you don't know how to have the event make more money.

2. Why are you really having the event, anyway?

   This may not be the "official" reason you tell the world, but what would insiders say is the real reason you are having this event? Is it because no one could say no to the board chair or a key volunteer? Is it just the habitual thing to do?

3. Is there really an expectation this event will raise money? If so, is the stated fund-raising goal for the event different from

the amount you absolutely must raise from the event? Is everyone expecting it will raise the amount you put in the budget?

4. How attached are you to the form of this event—annual dinner, auction, etc.? How attached are the others who are involved? Do they know the facts about how little it nets for the amount of work it takes to produce?

5. What if someone just walked in and wrote you a check for your total goal? Would you still have the event? Pretend for a moment, that you alone had the power to kill each event. If you knew you had the money goal covered, which ones would you ax?

6. Thinking ahead to your next big event, if you don't make your goal, what will be the reason? It is interesting to notice you probably already know what the reasons and excuses will be, yet continue to go through the motions.

7. If the event is supposed to be a fund raiser, do you know how much it actually nets? Has anyone actually calculated the true costs, adding in all the staff costs in addition to volunteer time and the obvious hard costs?

8. How many volunteers did it really take to put the event on? Did you burn them out or make them happy? Are they bored with the event? Would they rather have hosted a little gathering and had you and a "testimonial person" come and tell your story? Would they rather have just given you a check and skipped the event altogether?

9. If you have dedicated fund-raising staff, what else could they have been doing with the same amount of time and energy to bring in more money than the event nets? For example, what if they spent the same number of hours making calls or visits to major donors? What might that have yielded?

10. For how many months in advance have you and your team been obsessing about the event? What about the terror the weeks and days before the event approaches, or the fear of

whether you will even make the break-even number, assuming you know what that number is?

11. Speaking of break even, do you know from the beginning you have big fixed costs to meet? These are things like theater ticket sales, pricey food costs, audio/visual equipment, room rental costs—anything you couldn't get donated.

12. What about the trade-offs with the donors? Getting a corporate underwriter for $1,000 to $5,000 may be a lot easier than going after that big gift with the same corporation, yet it may let them off the hook for a lot less. What about the risk of several of your volunteers asking the same corporation for a gift, thereby confusing them and again getting you less than the ultimate gift?

13. Is this the right kind of event for your organization? Is it consistent with your mission? How could it showcase your mission even more? Is it the best way to tell your organization's story?

14. Does this type of event give you enough predictors of the results? Are there enough benchmarks along the way to let you adjust accordingly in advance if you have fewer Table Captains or tickets sold?

15. What would you think if you had to sit through that program? Do people really care about the speaker? Is the speaker's message even relevant to your organization or is the speaker just there to draw in more guests? If the latter, then how many more people will that speaker attract? How much more in the bottom line? Will that extra revenue more than cover the speaker's fees? What is the likelihood those guests who come just to hear this speaker will ever become lifelong donors?

16. What are you building for future years by having this event? Where does this event fit into your overall individual giving program?

If you have taken the time to tell the truth about each of your events, you should have a good sense of which ones you are committed to keeping or dropping. Now let's see how to retool them to build you more lifelong donors.

CHAPTER 20

PLANNING EVENTS: BEGIN WITH THE FOLLOW UP

Although it seems counter-intuitive, the first thing to consider as you redesign each of your events to grow your base of lifelong donors is the follow up. This is true whether the event is destined to become a Point of Entry, a Free Feel-Good Cultivation Event, or a One-Hour Asking Event. You must plan the entire event working backwards from your plan for follow up.

What is it about your organization that you want the guests to remember? What will you want them to say when they receive their personal Follow-Up Call?

How will you decide which of the guests you can legitimately follow up with without it feeling too pushy? In other words, what will be your tracking system at the event for identifying people who really would like to stay in contact with you? How will they let you know that you have their permission to contact them?

The easiest and most up-front method is to have some sort of reply card the guests can fill out and give back to a designated person, ideally their table host, indicating they would like more information about your program. While this is clearly the most straightforward, even those who are very interested may be reluctant to be the only person at their table who is filling out such a card.

Another approach that works well is to have the emcee, or some other key person who is part of the official program, tell the audience, after the Facts and Emotional Hook have been presented, something like this:

> "While we know that most of you just came today to play golf (or dance or whatever), you may have discovered during our program that you have an interest in learning more about our work. There is a person seated at each table who is very familiar with our organization. For today, they are serving as our experts. Would that person at each table please raise your hands now so we can all see who you are? (Pauses while hands go up and everyone looks around.) Feel free to talk with them and let them know you'd like more information. We would be delighted to have someone from the organization talk with you further."

That kind of a statement sets you up pretty well to capture the next tier of interested guests.

Of course, you give these designated experts special ribbons on their name tags and make a big fuss about them. Let them know in advance that you are counting on them to circulate and talk to as many people as they can during the event. Tell them you will be calling them to debrief the day after the event. In other words, they should be on their toes during the entire event.

A third approach is to get a little more gutsy and see whom you could call quite naturally even if they did not give you explicit permission to do so. If any of the guests were prior "insiders" —donors, volunteers or board members— you should assume you already have enough implicit permission to call them randomly and ask for their frank feedback about the event. Also ask them about any other comments or reactions they heard from other guests. They will be flattered that you considered them enough of an insider to call.

A fourth strategy is to review the various categories of guests in terms of their past association with your organization or in terms of the role they played in the event and then call two or three key people in each category to help you with your "random follow-up survey." While it is a bit contrived, people will be impressed you are taking the time to solicit their input and most will be delighted to talk with you. As you listen to their responses, see if you can sniff out any trends you might want to pursue with a telephone or email campaign to a broader group of attendees.

Lastly, consider the guests who said they wanted to attend but did not attend. How could you legitimately follow up with them? If a personal phone call seems like too much, could you send them a copy of the video with a "We missed you " note from their friend?

Everyone who will be involved in the follow-up process needs to be well setup from the beginning. They are your undercover agents during the event. Deputize your board members and long-term supporters. Have them keep their antennae up.

What Kind of Follow Up and When?

The top secret of follow up in the new reality is timing.

The two weeks after each event is, by far, the most fertile time for additional fund raising as well as cultivation. For most event organizers, by the time the actual event happens, they are burned out and exhausted. Your guests, on the other hand, are just getting interested. Now is the time they are curious and eager to learn more. Tell your event planners and key development staff not to schedule their vacations until at least two weeks after the event. Otherwise they miss the delayed culmination of their work.

In terms of the type of follow up, you have no doubt already thought of the obvious: letters. Most organizations have gotten the thank-you letter down to an art form. It is a beautifully-crafted letter, personally signed by the perfect person. Ideally suited to the pace of the old reality, it arrives a week or two after the event. By then, you will be lucky if many of your guests even remember having attended. In other words, in the new reality, letters are fine for the formal IRS-required response, but they will not get you that timely, open-ended feedback you need.

Your first choice should be the telephone because it provides immediate, voice-to-voice, real-time dialog. Although many of your donors may prefer email, for the majority nothing yet substitutes for a phone call or a voice mail message left within three days of the event, while the afterglow is still warm. This call or message thanks the person for coming and asks for their feedback, again engaging them directly with a real person associated with your organization. Speaking of messages, yes, it is fine to leave a voice mail or send an email message. Let them know how to reach you and be prepared to call them two more times to actually connect with them.

All of this phone contact requires that you did an impeccable job of capturing the names and phone numbers of the guests at your event. If the event was well done, they will have left inspired and educated. In other words, they should still remember you. Since many of them gave someone their names to be called, they will have been looking forward to hearing from you.

Who Is the Best Person to Make the Follow-Up Call?

The best person to make the Follow-Up Call is someone very closely connected to your organization. Ideally this person is someone they met at the event, even in passing, who will be their ongoing contact over the next few years, their Donor Services Representative. In many cases, this will be one high-level staff person or a long-time volunteer who single handedly does all the follow up. This provides consistency for your guests. I recommend *not* having guests followed up by their personal friends, other than as a courtesy, thank-you call. This "official"

Follow-Up Call should be done by someone closer to the inside of the organization, yet at arms-length from the guests so they have the freedom to give more direct feedback.

The only exception to this is in the case of a very large event where a large number of guests will be receiving Follow-Up Calls. Then you will need many callers. In this case, assemble your best team or train the table experts to make the Follow-Up Calls.

The Script for the Follow-Up Call

Be sure that each caller is following the same script or outline of general questions you want to have covered. This will insure consistency. Also be sure they have a standardized way of recording the information so it can be entered into your data base right away.

Here is a basic script of what you will want to cover in the post-event Follow-Up Call. You will want to modify it to fit your situation.

1. Thank the person for coming to the event. Let them know your organization is honored they made it a priority to be there.

2. Ask them what they thought about the event. What did they like most about it? Do they feel they learned anything new about the organization? What suggestions would they have for changes or improvements?

3. Is there any way they might like to become more involved with the organization? If they have already been involved, listen carefully here for signs of renewed or increased interest.

4. Is there anyone who came to mind during the event they would suggest you contact or invite to a tour or other Point of Entry event?

5. If they requested any additional information, let them know how you will be providing that. Thank them for taking their time for this call.

Now that you are primed for the follow up, we are ready to consider converting exiting fund-raising events to Point of Entry events.

CHAPTER 21

CONVERTING EXISTING EVENTS TO POINTS OF ENTRY

Most of the fund-raising events you are now working so hard to produce in order to attract new donors can be converted to Point of Entry events with relatively little tweaking. Furthermore, if you want to gear the event for your existing donors, and you can get the event fully underwritten so it is free to attend, you will have a Free Feel-Good Cultivation Event. As long as you are going to do the work of bringing people together for events, why not have them leave educated and inspired about your fine programs? Otherwise, what have you built for the future?

Let's review the three essential components of a Point of Entry event:

1. People get the *facts* about your organization at the basic level.

2. They are *hooked* in and feel connected emotionally to your work.

3. You are able legitimately to *"capture" their names,* phone numbers, and email addresses.

Think of all the events and occasions where you could accomplish those three essential ingredients:

- A black tie gala
- An awards event or volunteer recognition event
- An anniversary event
- A open-air picnic or concert
- A golf tournament
- A community meeting where you are invited to speak
- One of your standard volunteer orientation meetings
- A concert or arts performance
- A parent orientation night

Let's take something pretty standard, say an awards event or volunteer recognition event. It is a standard annual dinner affair. People have paid a respectable ticket price to attend. Look at the existing format of the event. What is the location, the program? How long are the guests with you? What are they already expecting?

Perhaps you are already doing a perfect Point of Entry event without even recognizing it. If not, the addition of a relatively brief testimonial from an artist or arts patron or a well-served family member or client (either in-person, on video, or delivered by a third person such as a staff member) can be very effective.

One of the keys to a successful Point of Entry event is intertwining the Facts, the Emotional Hook and the need so that, before they know it, the audience has had an experience of it all. If you are giving awards, make them brief but moving and chock full of facts that tie each person's story back to the mission of the organization or to one particular aspect of a program.

A participant in one of the Raising More Money workshops did this brilliantly at an awards dinner honoring homeless women who had turned their lives around. The tables had been sold to corporate sponsors, many of whom had given their tickets away to others to fill up the tables. She simply assumed the guests were there not only to attend a lovely dinner but also to learn more about the organization. She started the program with some inspirational words from the emcee, the chief executive officer of the major corporate sponsor of the event. This was followed immediately by a moving video about the organization's work. Then the emcee encouraged people to enjoy their dinner and to spend some time talking with the special guest at their table who was most familiar with the organization—either a board member, volunteer or staff person. He also encouraged them to take a moment to read the "testimonial inserts" in their printed programs.

After dinner came the awards presentations, which had been well-scripted and served as real-life testimonials to these women's extraordinary accomplishments in the face of great obstacles. As each woman was called up to receive her award, she was asked to sit in one of the chairs on the stage. At the end of the awards, all the recipients were asked to stand. Of course, after hearing each woman's story, there was a standing ovation and not a dry eye in the house.

Board members were assigned clusters of tables to visit after the dessert was served. The executive director had briefed the table hosts on the overall objective for the event. "This isn't just a pretty party. We want to be sure every single guest leaves here tonight knowing more about our organization, both the facts and the emotional impact of the work we do." Table Captains, staff and board members all knew in advance that the development staff would call them to debrief on Monday morning. They knew to be on the lookout for people who expressed a real interest in the cause. And before the evening ended, the emcee invited the guests to leave their business card or let their Table Captain know if they would like more information about the organization.

Within a week, every guest who expressed any sincere interest in the organization had received a follow-up call from the director of development. This was in addition to the standard thank-you call or note that their table host would naturally do.

Many people asked if they could take a tour of the shelter (which became their real Point of Entry event). Others offered in-kind or cash gifts. Some wanted to host a Point of Entry event of their own. Because this organization was planning to do a Free One-Hour Asking Event, they were able to convert many awards dinner guests to Table Captains for the upcoming asking event. The organization raised more than $300,000 at their black tie gala as well as generating a passion and commitment that led to many new Table Captains for their bigger asking event. Good strategy!

Remember, whatever your event, this will most likely be the only opportunity you will ever have to tell your story to some of these people. Start by having your board chair say something like, "We know most of you came here tonight to have a lovely dinner and time to socialize, but we at the City Women's Shelter would not be doing our jobs if we did not take the opportunity while we have you all assembled to give you some first-hand examples of our work."

In no more than 10 minutes, you can convert your basic gala into a Point of Entry event and you will have gotten the job done. People will leave feeling they were a part of something bigger than themselves. If someone were to give them a pop quiz the next morning, they should be able to remember the name of your organization and at least one anecdote about your programs and services. If you do your job right, most likely they also will remember the testimonials and a few choice statistics.

Finally, don't forget the third essential ingredient: Capturing the Names of those who want more information. Most events enable you to gather that kind of information easily, although not always. The golf tournament and even the Rotary or Lions Clubs may not be forthcoming with names. And no captured names means no Point of Entry event. That doesn't mean you should decline those speaking engagements. Just know that you won't be able to do the one-to-one follow up necessary to build a lifelong donor.

On the other hand, when people who come up to you at the end of your Rotary presentation full of passion for your cause, be sure to ask for their card and give them yours. You can count them as having attended a Point of Entry event, make the Follow-Up Call, and take them around the cycle if they are truly interested.

CHAPTER 22

FREE FEEL-GOOD CULTIVATION EVENTS

The third type of event is the Free Feel-Good Cultivation Event, also known as a Point of Re-Entry Event.

If you have the costs underwritten, the event can be provided at no cost to the donors. Many of the events you now have will fall into this category. These events are aimed at prior donors as a "reward" for their loyal support. They powerfully reconnect the donor to the mission of the organization and reinforce their original decision to give. Donors leave feeling good, saying to themselves: "I'm glad I give money there. I will keep doing that. Maybe I could give more."

No one is asked to give at these events. They are strictly a reward and reinforcement event. When Point of Re-Entry Events are done in conjunction with the multiple-year gift-club levels, you can encourage prior donors to invite 'new' people to these events. For the new people, the event will be a Point of Entry.

Let's look at some examples:

The donor recognition dinner is the classic example of a Free Feel-Good Cultivation Event. All donors at a certain level are invited to a special home or boat or garden where they are thanked, honored and reconnected to the facts and emotional impact of your work. Let the guests know in advance there will be a short program.

Begin with a welcome and thank you from one of your key board members. Plaques may be presented to each donor or something more personal such as a framed children's drawing. Then be sure you include at least one live testimonial from a client, family member, volunteer or staff member—and make it good.

Next the visionary leader briefs the donors on the state of the organization for no more than five minutes, telling them how far you have come thanks to their help. Then the leader paints the picture of the organization's future, the next phase of the dream, the next level of needs. This can border on a "soft" Ask. "We're looking forward to building our own building in the next three years. You'll be hearing more about that as the time comes closer."

The visionary leader can even mention a Challenge Gift that has been received or better yet, announce the challenge now to these donors as insiders. If the donors to the Challenge Gift Fund are present, have them say what inspired them to contribute in this way. It will help launch the next phase of the campaign and encourage people to increase their gifts. It is fine to have the visionary leader or board member say, "We are still looking for other gifts to be added to this pool of Challenge Funds." That way no one will feel left out.

Notice all this is strictly informational. No one is being asked. After all, these donors are your inside family. If you were part of the family, you would not want to hear about this big news indirectly. You would want to be among the first to know. Perhaps you would have an opinion about it.

With your loyal donors, the issue is not when and how to ask them to give, but making sure you don't offend them by inadvertently overlooking them in some way. This is where your ongoing follow up pays off. Someone knows those donors well enough to be able to anticipate how the program at your Free Feel-Good Cultivation Event will sound to them. It is as if you could do a dress rehearsal of the event and know how everyone in the audience will receive and interpret the information.

The entire program for this event should last no more than 30 minutes. Then give people plenty of time to mix and mingle. The networking effect of these events is magical. Be sure the crowd is interspersed with board and staff members who can give you feedback on each guest the next day. Since this is a Point of Re-Entry Event, you will be starting the cycle with them again by making Follow-Up Calls.

Another type of Free Feel-Good Cultivation Event is inviting your existing donors to some regularly scheduled event with your clients. Maybe donors are invited to the reunion with parents and premature babies hosted every other year by the hospital. Now that would be a tear-jerker! It could be preceded by a special reception for donors with the head physician in the pediatrics unit and the head of the hospital. Or donors are invited to the regularly-scheduled graduation, preceded by a special reception with the principal and board.

A third example of a Free Feel-Good Cultivation or Point of Re-Entry Event is a private, issue-oriented forum with a sought-after speaker. This works well for policy and national organizations and can be taken on the road. Just be sure to include enough emotion in the testimonials and the impassioned dream of the visionary leader. Otherwise you will have an intellectual evening, which is not sufficient for a Free Feel-Good Cultivation Event.

Launching a Volunteer Giving Program

A fourth example of a Free Feel-Good Event is a volunteer recognition event. When planned as a Point of Re-Entry, it can be used to launch a volunteer-driven volunteer giving program. Here is a suggested road map:

Begin by identifying two or three key volunteers who are supportive of the notion of volunteer giving. Ask them to co-chair your next volunteer recognition event or serve on the Event Committee.

Then design that event to be a powerful Point of Re-Entry for your volunteers. Give people sufficient facts about your current programs and needs. Be sure to show a video or provide enough of an emotional testimonial that people will be reconnected to the mission. As you present the awards to selected volunteers, highlight the many aspects of your programs in which volunteers play essential roles.

Within three days after the event, have your Co-Chairs or Event Committee personally call as many of the guests as possible. Use the standard Follow-Up script (see pages 121-122) to thank them and ask for their feedback.

Then have the follow-up caller add the following:

"You know, after a wonderful event like that, many of us have been thinking about how we, as volunteers, can help the organization to expand its programs to those areas of need we see so clearly. We don't know whether we would start some type of special fund or give at one of the levels already designed for this. Would you have an interest in being involved in something like that?"

Have the phoners write up their notes on each call. Then summarize the results. What percentage seem generally favorable? Neutral? Negative? Assuming that the 20-60-20 rule will hold true, you will have 20% of the people saying they are favorable, 60% neutral and 20% opposed.

Next, design your Units of Service or giving levels. Try to avoid adding different levels to the giving levels the organization already has. Make sure the donors understand these categories are for unrestricted operating funds.

Then move forward with your Asks, all to be done by active, well-respected volunteers. Either by letter or email, by phone or in person, they explain to the volunteers that, based on the feedback received, many volunteers have expressed an interest in becoming sustaining financial supporters of the organization. They invite the volunteer/donor to join them in participating at whatever level would be comfortable for them.

Organize another Free Feel-Good Cultivation Event within three months of the asks to showcase the kinds of things their money has provided. Encourage the volunteers/donors to bring friends, family and other volunteers to join them. Whether the event is a Science Fair to showoff the expanded science programs, a lecture from a noted thinker in your issue area, or a "welcome" reception for the new staff person hired as a result of that extra funding, let the donors in on the good news. Treat them as the true insiders they are.

After each event, have their Donor Service Representative follow up with them again, personally, to get their feedback and advice. Keep inviting, following-up, listening and asking. Keep customizing each step to what they are telling you they want. Keep treating them as the new breed of Volunteer/Donor. They will grow into major lifelong donors.

CHAPTER 23

THE FREE ONE-HOUR
ASKING EVENT

The third category of event is the Free One-Hour Asking Event. As the name implies, we actually ask people to give money at this event.

If people have already paid a ticket price, regardless of how small a price, they will resent being asked to give any additional money at the event. In their minds, they have already given. The price of their ticket was their gift to you. Even in the case of an auction, a raffle, or a golf tournament, where donors are getting plenty of tangible goodies in return, most donors will feel any money spent was their contribution to their organization.

In our model, to qualify as an Asking Event, there is no ticket price to the guest. That is right, it is a *free* Asking Event. People know in advance they will be asked to give. Yet they are not required to give at all. There are no minimum and no maximum gifts suggested. In other words, people can give nothing.

This format is now used for many highly successful events, including one that annually raises over $1 million in one hour. Compared to most events people are now busy producing, this type of event requires significantly less work. The best part about it, besides the bottom-line of course, is that the entire hour is spent educating the audience about your programs. It is a large-group Point of Entry event, ideally for people who have already been to a Point of Entry. The big difference is that this time they are asked to give at specified Units of Service for Multiple Years.

Let's look at how it works.

You have done your Point of Entry events. You have followed up, in many cases several times, with the same person. You can identify with the help of your data base a core group of people who are passionate about the work of your organization. They may not be the people with the most money or the best contacts, but they *love* your organization. You call them and ask if they would consider being a Table Captain at your free breakfast (or lunch) fund-raising event four to six months from now.

They are flattered yet confused. "Free breakfast fund-raising event?" they ask. "Just what does that mean?"

"That's right", you reply. "There's no charge to you for being a Table Captain, and no charge to any of your guests for attending. It's absolutely free. Yes, they will be asked to contribute, but there will be no minimum and no maximum. I repeat, no minimum. They can give any amount they like. It will be our job to inspire them to want to give. As much as anything, we want people to come and find out about our organization."

Let's say 30 people agree to be Table Captains. Their job is to fill a table of 10 on the day of the event. That means they will need to start by inviting many more than 10 guests and by confirming at least 14 people personally (with reminder postcards and phone calls) at least twice as the event approaches, including once the day before the event. That is what it will take to produce 10 people at their table on the day of the event.

On the morning of the event, the Table Captains arrive early to greet their guests. The guests arrive, somewhat confused, wondering what this is all about, looking for the coffee. Though they have been told this is a one-hour event, no one believes it. People are assuming they will need to slip out a little early, write a check, and get back to their workplace.

Instead, you wake them up, dazzle them, inspire them, and then ask for their money, all within 60 minutes. In this world of instant gratification, given the rate at which things zip by, you have got to be able to make an indelible impact on people in 60 minutes or less. They need to see right away that this organization is different. From the moment they get out of their cars at the front of the hotel or restaurant, you have to shake up their reality by having someone there to greet them—real people who are a part of your organization, staff, students, volunteers, whoever is appropriate.

To illustrate not just the greeting but the entire event process, I'll use another example from Zion Preparatory Academy, the extraordinary, inner-city, private academy that has used this event several years in a row, reaping great rewards.

(NOTE: Do not be dissuaded from trying this type of event if your organization does not have cute kids to show off and talk about. The format of this event can easily be modified for all types of organizations, including national policy organizations, arts organizations, professional associations, etc.)

As you get out of your car at the front door of the hotel, there to greet you are two elementary school students, holding hands. Dressed in their plaid uniforms, bright-eyed and freshly scrubbed, they greet you with big smiles. "Good morning, welcome to the breakfast event; thank you for coming; just go right this way." You enter the hotel to find another pair of students who shake your hand, welcome you, and guide you up the escalator to the mezzanine level where the ballroom is located.

As you ride up the escalator wondering what this is all about, you hear music. You can't see the ballroom yet, but you can hear the voices of a children's choir, accompanied by an organ, singing rousing songs that put you in the mood. You arrive at the ballroom level, find your name tag with your table number on a table in the lobby, and hurry in to find your table. You greet your friend the Table Captain and find your place.

At the stroke of 7:30 a.m., the event begins, as scheduled. While generally only 60% of the guests are on time, this event is orchestrated like a space shuttle launch and every minute counts. Although people are still arriving, you start on time with the perfunctory welcome to everyone by the board chair who also thanks the board members, the Table Captains, and other visiting dignitaries. To add another taste of your mission, there is an invocation delivered by a pastor and child.

Then the board chair tells everyone, "Enjoy your breakfast. We'll be back to start the program in about 10 minutes." You must give people time to be social with the other people at their table. Otherwise, people will feel they are being rude. Yet given that every single one of our 60 minutes counts, you want to use this 10 minutes of "down time" to forward the crescendo you are building toward.

As you are eating your breakfast (a cold breakfast with the tables already set with lots of food, including hot coffee), talking to the person next to you, you feel a tap on your shoulder. You turn around to see a child holding a basket of apples, offering you one. "Thank you for coming today, would you like an apple?" It happens so fast that, for most of the guests, the impact is almost subliminal, yet people do remember: This is a real child who goes to this school. This is a child who could benefit if I give money today.

Also, as you are eating your breakfast, people start noticing the drawings in the center of the tables or inserted in their programs. On half-sized paper are crayon drawings of what each child wants to be when he or she grows up. They have written below the drawings, in their own words, "I want to be a teacher, a scientist, a pilot, etc." These "centerpieces" become conversation pieces at the tables and people take them home as mementoes of the event.

The program begins again. Similar to the Point of Entry event which more than half these guests have already attended, the visionary leader speaks in a very inspiring way for seven minutes about the mission, the philosophy, and why the work of this school is so essential. The visionary leader then introduces the video, a seven-minute virtual tour of the school, including testimonials from students, parents and teachers. The video moves people to tears several times as it drives home the message. The lights come back on, gradually.

Next on the agenda are testimonials that begin with the school choir singing two songs, quickly and adorably. There is nothing quite like the sound of kids voices singing to inspire people. Then, while they are still assembled on the risers on the stage, children in the choir are interviewed by a well-know local media personality. Holding her microphone to their faces one by one, she asks: "Why do you like going to this school?"

"Oh, my teacher, I love my teacher."

"The hugs I get in the morning."

"The food; I love the food."

Next question: "What's your favorite subject?"

"Math"

"Science"

"Math"

"Math"

"Reading"

And finally: "What do you want to be when you grow up?" This is where the audience melts. Here are little children, belting out in their loudest voices, not what they want to be, but what they are going to be. The children start saying the kinds of things they had written on their drawings at the tables:

"I'm going to be a scientist."

"A teacher."

"An engineer."

In that moment, even if you have never heard of this school before and have only come because your friend the Table Captain invited you, you are moved. You can see that whether or not they ever become a pilot or teacher, each child has a vision and a dream for their lives. Given the statistics you heard during the presentation and the video, you know it is not a foregone conclusion that each of these children will grow up with the likelihood of a bright future. You can see and feel that something is happening at this school that is changing lives. If you are ever going to make a contribution to a program like this, this school definitely seems to know what it is doing. It would be a good investment.

Next on the program (now 50 minutes into the hour) is the "pitch" person—perhaps a Chairman of the Board of a major corporation, someone with a lot of credibility, or someone closely connected to the mission of the organization, even a family member. Knowing that by now the audience is well warmed-up, he does not need to convince people to give. In fact, any more convincing would cause overripe fruit. His job is to ask in a very straightforward manner.

When we go to an Asking Event, we know what is coming. As this person gets up to do the pitch, people are already thinking about how much they can give. "What will my spouse or partner say?" "How much room is on my credit card?" At this point, each of us tends to get very focused on ourselves and to stop paying attention to the speaker. That is why smart "pitch" people know that, at this point in the event, their job is to just walk people through the pledge card step-by-step.

He introduces himself, saying he is part of the fund-raising board of the school. "I love this school. In the last hour, you have met our students, you have seen our programs. My job today is to ask for your support. I'd like to ask the Table Captains to pass out the pledge cards now." Note that the pledge cards were not waiting at your place when you arrived for breakfast. If they had been, many people would have filled them out before they had absorbed the program and some might have left early.

He pauses while the pledge cards are distributed. "Now we know that most of you had no idea what we were going to ask you for today. You came because your friend invited you. And others of you are already familiar with the school. Perhaps you've taken one of our tours. When we looked at what we wanted to ask you for today, we decided to ask for what we really need. We have approximately 600 students at the school. Parents and family members work hard to pay the tuition. Yet there is still a gap. Our shortfall each year is $600,000.

RAISING MORE MONEY®

Sample Pledge Card Wording

(Organization name) can count on my support!

Date _____

Name _____

Organization _____

Address _____

City _____ State _____ Zip _____

Day Phone _____

Evening Phone _____

E-mail _____

I would like to:

❑ Sponsor _____ Children: $1,000 per year for 5 years

❑ Sponsor _____ Group Homes: $25,000 per year for 5 years

❑ Endow a place for a child: $20,000 (to be paid over _____ years)

❑ Contribute $ _____ for _____ years

❑ Please contact me: I have other thoughts to share.

Payment:

❑ My check is enclosed, made payable to: _____

❑ Please charge my Visa/MC #_____ exp. _____

❑ My company will match my gift

We will bill you every November for your annual pledge unless you request otherwise:

_____

"Today we're asking those of you who can make a contribution of $1,000 a year to Sponsor a Student by pledging to do that for the next 5 years. It will provide stability for our students and the school administration to know that you'll be doing that for five years. One thousand dollars is $83 a month. Please check off the first box on the pledge card if you can do that."

"This is not a scholarship program. Your money does not go directly to a particular student. As much as anything, these categories are just gimmicks to have people feel connected to our school. All of the money raised today supports the general operations of the school, to enable the staff to continue doing the outstanding work you've seen here today."

He pauses between each category to give people a chance to fill out the card. Then he says, "Some of you are capable of giving more. You may have a corporation, a family foundation, or just the capacity to give at a larger level. We have 25 students in each classroom. We'd like you to consider giving $25,000 a year for the next five years to Sponsor a Classroom of students. If you can do that, check the second box.

"Now, some of you who can do that may want to become involved with a particular classroom of kids, and stay with them over the next five years. You may want to have your staff or family come out and put on parties or do special projects. That's great. Others of you may not want to get involved that directly. You're happy just to give the money to support this classroom. That's fine, too.

"Moving down to the next box on your form: Some of you don't like giving to operating needs. You'd rather give to an endowment fund. If you give a gift of $20,000, or $5,000 a year for four years, we'll put that money in an investment account. We figure, conservatively, it will earn 5% interest. That annual interest equals $1,000 a year (the same amount as the first category, the Sponsor a Student category). You would be Endowing a (place for a) Student forever."

He pauses to catch his breath and repeats, "We know most of you did not know how much we were going to ask you for today. You came because your friend invited you. We started by asking you to give in these larger categories. I hope that many of you have chosen to do that.

"Now, I'd like to ask those of you who have not yet given to tell us how much you'd like to give and for how long. The fourth box on the pledge card lets you do that. Whatever you can give, we truly appreciate." (Note: This is the fill-in-the-blanks category, letting the donor determine their own giving level and number of years. See sample pledge card on page 209.)

"Finally, perhaps you want more information, would like to take a tour of the school, etc. Please check the last box, the one that says: 'Please contact me, I have other thoughts to share.' Thank you again for your support for our children." He pauses to give the guests several minutes to fill out the form. Then he turns the program over to the emcee to wrap it up.

Sixty-minutes and the event is over. People are inspired. They linger to talk to friends. A tape of the children singing is playing in the background.

In the space of that hour, more than $1 million has been raised, including pledges. People have not felt pressured. The people who gave are glad they did. The people who didn't give (about 12%) do not feel uncomfortable about not giving.

About half the guests had already been to a Point of Entry tour at the school. They had received Follow-Up Calls and many had become involved. For the other half of the guests, this event was their Point of Entry event. After all, it contained the Facts, the Emotional Hook, and a mechanism for Capturing the Names. Some guests jumped right in and gave anyway. Others were just absorbing the first round of information.

Summary

Let's review the major points about the Free One-Hour Asking Event. First, it needs to be free. For the event just described, had there been any admission charge for the breakfast, the event would not have been nearly as successful. In the new reality, the free event allows people the freedom to choose, and as a result they will give more generously.

Second, remember the two key ingredients of any Ask: Units of Service and the Multiple-Year Pledges. Looking at the event for the school, consider this: What if, after all that outstanding work been done to educate and inspire people, instead of asking for specific amounts, the "pitch" person had said: "Please give generously. We ask you to give from the bottom of your hearts."

What does that mean? In this day and age, people need specific categories. Otherwise, those who are highly capable of giving will give less. And those with less giving capacity will give less. Without specific giving categories, you will have put all that work into an event that could have brought in more than a million dollars and you may find yourself settling for $20,000 or $30,000.

Likewise, why not ask for a Multiple-Year Pledge? These people have gone to all the trouble to get there. They have sat through your outstanding program. They were genuinely moved to contribute. Why not seize the moment and ask them to commit to give for several years? Only those who make the multiple-year commitment are listed in the Sponsor-a-Student Society. Of course it is fine if people want to give $1,000 for one year only. That will not qualify them, however, to be in the Multiple-Year Giving Society. If you can get your nerve up to ask for Multiple Years, you will not regret it. If anything, as the fifth year rolls around, you will wish you had asked people to give for 10 years, not five.

Frequently Asked Questions About the Free One-Hour Asking Event

Q: *What percentage of five-year pledges from this event did people actually pay off?*

A: The rate of pledges paid was just about 95%. While that might sound exceptionally high, put yourself in that donor's shoes. We kept in touch with each of those donors on a highly personalized basis. They never again became strangers. They only became closer friends of the family. In addition to being invited to two Free Feel-Good Cultivation Events during the year, all the multiple-year donors were invited to attend the Free One-Hour Asking Event each year as well. Many chose to become Table Captains in subsequent years. By inviting their own friends and family to the event, they were deepening their own resolve about the good work of the organization. Not paying off their pledge was never a consideration for the great majority of these donors.

Q: *Did your giving levels preclude your going back and asking those same donors for larger gifts before the five years had passed?*

A: During the "pitch" in each subsequent year, the multiple-year donors were asked to increase their pledges. Rather than merely paying their second year's pledge payment at the event, the biggest surprise was the number of people who paid off the remaining balance on their five-year pledge and then pledged to sponsor one, two or more students again.

Q: *You started with a pretty large event. Our group will be skeptical about this approach. Is it possible to start off smaller?*

A: Yes, absolutely. The minimum recommended size is 10 Table Captains, or an event for 100 people. Most organizations can come up with the names of 10 people who would be willing to give this approach a try. If you start small the first year, all the skeptics will be watching to see how much money you raise. Once they see the results, compared to the amount of work it takes to put on the other big events you have been offering, they will become converts.

Q: *What about the one or two fabulous volunteers whose lives revolve around organizing our annual auction or dinner? How do we wean them from the old-style events and convert them to supporters of the Free One-Hour Asking Event?*

A: Those volunteers are very smart and very loyal. They will want you to do whatever raises the most money for the organization, but not until they see it produce. Those wonderful events they have been organizing should be retooled to become Points of Entry or underwritten to become Free Feel-Good Cultivation Events.

Q: *This event sounds too good to be true. Our organization already has plenty of loyal donors. Do we have to take the time to bring everyone to a Point of Entry before we can put on the Free One-Hour Asking Event?*

A: No, you can definitely shortcut the process. Go back to your Treasure Map and identify as many people as you can from each category (board, volunteers, staff, vendors, etc) who would be willing to serve as Table Captains for your first event.

Then invite *them* to a Point of Entry event if they need to be freshly reconnected. In your Follow-Up Call after the Point of Entry event, tell them you are planning to put on this event, explain how it works, and ask if they, as a loyal supporter, would consider being a Table Captain.

Try It

As we conclude this section on special events, I hope you will consider trying the Free One-Hour Asking Event. Most groups are a bit skeptical at first. The biggest concern is that people think their friends will feel pressure to give money at the event. Once they see how naturally the hour flows, how some people give and some do not, how the event educates the guests and builds true friends for the organization while raising more money than most of the other special events combined, they will become believers.

So set the date for the big event and get to work!

CHAPTER 24

TAKING THE RAISING MORE MONEY MODEL ONLINE

Now that you are becoming more comfortable with the landscape of the new reality and you are armed with a system for building lifelong donors, you can begin to see how to adapt this approach to all kinds of venues. Given the pivotal role that online giving will play in the years to come, let's look at how to use our model to conduct a fully-online program.

While this may still seem premature, at the rate things are changing, you had best get prepared. Over the next five to ten years the Internet will become the most frequently used mode of giving.

For many organizations, this is already true. The majority of their existing donors prefer giving online. To save time, travel or to avoid human contact, even your loyal local donors may find it easier to click money your way than to write you a check. You will be surprised to find how many of your existing loyal donors may switch to online giving when you make it available to them.

The more obvious application for online giving, of course, is for reaching distant donors and potential donors. If your organization has a regional, national or international presence, the Internet brings everyone closer. You can create an instant community of donors and supporters, link them to you and to one another to chat about whatever you like.

Remember that online "giving" is only one aspect of the lifelong relationship you are aiming to develop by using this model. While it is certainly possible to use the Internet merely to drive money your way, it misses the rich opportunities this medium affords to cultivate a truer relationship. The Internet allows us to customize, personalize, connect and stay connected over time with a unique sense of immediacy. It is ideally suited to building lifelong donors. Let's look at how to walk through all four steps of the Raising More Money model online.

Step One: Point of Entry

If you spend any time visiting other nonprofit Web sites, you will quickly notice which ones grab you. A great Web site, when designed to include the three essential elements—Facts, Emotional Hook, and a legitimate way to Capture the Names of your guests—becomes a Point of Entry. Those boring dry sites will not do the trick. Nor will the ones with all the fancy streaming video of the disaster victims and hungry children. The front page of your Web site must contain both the Facts and the Emotional Hook. Just as with a live event, some of the best online Points of Entry I have seen use stories and testimonials, combined with still or moving photos and music, to hook you. Have it be a virtual walk-through or tour of your organization.

You can include the same three handouts used at a live Point of Entry: the Fact Sheet, the Wish List and your standard brochure. These can be easily linked to your front page or introduced at the right time in the click-through virtual tour.

Your online Point of Entry must leave people in the same place as your live Point of Entry, that is, having answered the questions: How does the work of this organization change lives? How does it affect the life of one person or one family?

Do not trust your own instincts to gauge the impact of your online Point of Entry. Test it out on a few people to see if it is strong enough to educate and inspire them. Odds are it will need more emotion. How many screens do they have to click through to get to the good stuff? Make it readily available once they arrive at your site.

How are you going to capture the names? The Internet is the home of permission marketing. You must have people's permission to give you their names and to stay in touch with them. And you have to earn that permission. Usually the way you earn it is by giving them something of value in return.

Your Web site, for example, will be educating them about a subject they want to know more about. If you have truly grabbed their interest, they will want to stay in contact with you. Have a box or page for them to type in their comments about your Web site (even anonymously) and then, if they are willing, to give you their name. Look at what else you could offer them. An online newsletter or chat room where they can dialog with others may be of great interest. In exchange for offering that, you certainly have enough permission to ask for their contact information: name, organization, address, phone number and, of course, email address.

Step Two: Follow Up and Involve

Once you have their names, you are ready to go around the cycle. The next step is Follow Up. You have several options as to how to follow up.

Assuming you want to stay online, you can respond immediately with a standardized yet personalized email survey or questionnaire which thanks them for visiting your site and then asks them to answer the three follow-up questions:

- What did you think of our Web site and our organization (our online Point of Entry)?

- Is there any way you could see yourself becoming involved? Would you like to attend one of our get-acquainted events?

- Is there anyone else you can think of who might want to visit our site, take a live tour, or talk to us in person?

Or, you can select a subgroup of visitors to get more personal with. Email them yourself, one-on-one, in a slightly more chatty way and tell them you are trying to get people's feedback about your site. How did they locate your site in the first place? What worked about it for them? What were the barriers to using it? In other words, do not ask them all the questions you would ask in a standardized questionnaire format. Ask them one or two at a time and wait for their responses before asking for more. Your goal is to get a true dialog going with each person—to have it feel, to you and to them, as though there is a real person on the other side of the screen.

While, with many of your donors, your objective will be to get "live," in other words to switch to the telephone or face-to-face contact, you must respect online etiquette and earn that permission, step-by-step. Do not be tempted to overstep your bounds.

An obvious next step after an online dialog has been established, would be to invite the person to one of your live Point of Entry events. While you could post that as an open invitation on the front page of your Web site, whether or not people even go through your online Point of Entry, you will be much more likely to have people actually show up if they have already gotten to know you online.

Just like your telephone Follow-Up Calls, your job in the online follow up is to listen for the cues to each person's hot buttons. What is it about your work that captures their hearts? What experience in their lives led them to you? Is there anything in particular they would like more information about?

The online follow up must establish enough permission for you to re-contact them about a topic of their choosing. Ask them in your email dialog if they would like to subscribe to your newsletter. Would they prefer to receive it online? Perhaps they would like to come in to hear a lecture or some other mission-relevant event?

If they are a long distance away, what else can you offer them? Just the dialog or chat rooms or online news may be sufficient. Others may want a face-to-face visit when your Alumni Relations person comes to their town.

Determine the number or quality of contacts you will have with each potential donor before you ask them for money.

Step Three: Asking for Money

Just as with our live model, the virtual Ask must not be made until the fruit has ripened. Spend enough time on the Cultivation Superhighway to hasten the ripening. Keep providing whatever information or services each potential donor wants. Stay in "touch"!

When you are ready to ask for money, remember to include the same ingredients of a live, mail or telephone Ask: Units of Service and Multiple-Year Pledges. These can easily be done online.

Using the same gift levels and for the same number of years, invite your online potential donors to consider joining your Multiple-Year Society online.

This can be done in an email with a personalized invitation to give. Include your standard pledge card right in the email message or link your donors to the secured portion of your site. Let them fill it out right there and email it back to you if you have a way of taking secured donations, or have them print it out and fax it to you.

Be sure to stress the importance of making a Multiple-Year Pledge. Let them know that long-term financial stability of the organization is your first priority. They can help to be a part of that.

As we said in Chapter 7, it is not necessary that you go to the work and expense of setting up your own secured site. Talk with other providers of this service and contract it out. For a small fee, or none at all, they can save you ever having to get on the no-win treadmill of establishing your own internal mechanisms.

Online Free Feel-Good Cultivation Events

As soon as people have given, they are invited to a Free Feel-Good Cultivation Event, either live or virtual. Regardless of the venue, it must reconnect them to the Facts and Emotional Hook. It serves to reinforce their wise investment in your organization.

Granted, many online donors will not want to dress up and drive over. They have made it perfectly clear that their preferred medium for communicating with you is online. For those donors, their Free Feel-Good Event can be an online summary of all the people who have benefitted from your program, accompanied by a personal thank-you and testimonial letter from a child, adult, or staff member. You could even do an online drawing or other graphic acknowledgment.

Ask each donor to respond with a quote or comment just to let you know they received the message and that it resonated with them.

Include an online invitation to the live Free Feel-Good Cultivation Events.

One thing that will still be missing from this type of online Free Feel-Good Event is the reinforcing contact with other loyal donors. Think about how you can offer this virtual group experience to each donor. In some cases, the chat room or bulletin board will be helpful. In other cases, you may want to stage a virtual event in real time, where everyone logs on within a pre-arranged time span to hear testimonials and stories and to talk with each other. Depending on the scale of your organization, this may or may not be worthwhile. Many of the jumbo-sized national nonprofit organizations will find this very useful.

Just like in our live model, any Free Feel-Good Cultivation Event, or Point of Re-Entry, triggers another round of Follow

Up, each time getting more personal, deepening the permission and inviting the donor to real, live Points of Entry.

Step Four: Donors Introducing Others

Finally, these happy donors are invited to introduce others to the organization. Whether by sending them to the Web site Point of Entry or by inviting them to a live Point of Entry, this is a natural sign of a true believer in your cause: They will be so excited about your work they will want the other important people in their lives to get to know you.

Online giving does not let you off the hook in any way. It requires a relatively high level of comfort with the medium on your part as well as a relentless obsession with follow up. Without that, to reiterate, you have nothing more than a great online donor acquisition tool, or a tool for online "giving," as opposed to having a powerful system for acquiring and relating—for cultivating lifelong donors online.

CHAPTER 25

WORKING WITH BOARDS OF DIRECTORS IN THE NEW REALITY

This chapter contains some straight talk about boards, beginning with my own opinion that, overall, most nonprofit organizations are not nice enough to their board members.

In this new reality, where time is the most precious commodity, it is incredibly heartening to realize the amount of time and talent that people give to serve on boards. Yet, for whatever reason, even after we have worked so hard to recruit them, many of us take our board members for granted. Actually, it may be worse than that: We may feel they owe us something—more time, more hard work, more generous sharing of their contacts, etc. I say it is precisely this attitude that perpetuates the complaints about ineffective boards.

Take a minute to approach this from a different point of view. Put yourself in the board member's shoes. Think about the best experience you have ever had serving on a board. If you have never been a board member, then think about another type of volunteer experience, one where it seemed as if you could do no wrong.

Whatever you did just seemed to work brilliantly. You never felt the organization was taking advantage of you. You felt completely appreciated from the very beginning. In fact, they showered you with nice notes and appropriate little gifts and awards along the way. They took into consideration your other time commitments, they included your family in various activities. They honored your time and talents and gave you fun and challenging assignments. They supported you with great staff who made you look good and made sure the project was successful. They showcased your strengths and had others magically available to cover for your weaknesses. No doubt, you still have a warm feeling when you think about it.

Now think about what your board members would say if asked confidentially about their experience of serving on your board. How would it compare?

This is the Golden Rule of working with boards (and volunteers): Treat them only as you would want to be treated. Be even nicer to them than you are already being.

In those organizations where this is not the case, there is one simple thing missing. The staff have forgotten one of the most fundamental differences between staff members and board members: the board members are volunteers. They are *giving* you their time. It is a gift. They don't need to do this. Serving on your board is not their full-time job; they may already have one of those. This is an avocation, a small way of giving back to the community.

In most cases, board members do not want the day-to-day weight of the organization on their shoulders. That is what the staff are there for. They want to be kept informed and to be consulted for their wisdom and perspective. Their role is much more akin to a grandparent than a parent. It is a source of pleasure for them, not a burden or aggravation. When they go on vacation, they don't want to be worrying about your organization.

Furthermore, board members have radar for criticism. If they suspect in the slightest that you are being critical of them, they will retaliate—usually by leaving or by backing off significantly. As staff members, the sooner we understand this, the happier everyone will be.

In fairness to the staff, this dissonance between the roles of the staff and the board usually arises out of a wonderful relationship where the board member has provided invaluable assistance, most often on some very focused project that made a huge difference to the organization. The staff got hooked. They want more of that level of expertise and involvement from the board member. In some cases, they will get it, in others not.

Board members, like all volunteers, cannot always promise you a consistent level of time or energy. For many board members, your organization is a special project and they will work you into their lives and priorities as best they can. Focused, time-limited projects actually work quite well for board members if you clearly delineate the time commitment and staff support that will be available.

What if you and your staff were to commit yourselves to make working with your organization the single best volunteer experience each of your board members has ever had? Then you set about doing this by valuing them as the lifelong friend and supporter they will become, speaking to their most noble and generous qualities, and always reconnecting them to your mission. In other words, you treat them the very way you would treat any of your other lifelong major donors.

What if you committed to having your organization become so much a part of their lives, so much a part of who they are, that their satisfaction came from their involvement with you and was what they most wanted to be remembered for?

That is the stuff that real lifelong donors are made of.

I recommend you alter your expectations and begin regarding your board members as advocates for your work out there in their worlds. Treat them as your cherished ambassadors to the broader community. If a person of their stature and role did nothing more than speak well of your work in the community and educate people along the way, perhaps inviting them to take a tour, they would be getting their job done as board members.

Board Members and Fund Raising in the Old Reality

Let's walk through the experience of a board member in the old reality of fund raising.

First, someone in your organization probably spent a great deal of time recruiting each board member. They started by identifying the categories of expertise needed. For example, the organization could have been looking for someone with experience in human resources, real estate, human services, the arts, finance, or fund raising. Each potential board member was checked out thoroughly, courted, and then asked to join. You were thrilled when they accepted.

You had the board members read over the written agreement of what would be expected of them (also known as the job description). You made sure they digested all the fine print about their fund-raising responsibilities. Perhaps your organization has a minimum giving expectation for the board, or a "give, get, or get off" policy. Whatever your expectations, you made them clear up front before they agreed to serve.

Now, as your fresh and eager new recruit arrives at one of her first board meetings, ready to fill the 'CPA slot,' for example, one of the main agenda items is, of course, fund raising. It just happens to be the time of year for the big annual banquet, golf tournament, or fund drive. Before she has even gotten oriented to the basics of being on the board, the new member is being asked to do the part she dreaded most. Yes, she did know this was coming, and she did agree to help. So she takes a deep breath and scans her address book for her 10 closest friends or colleagues who cannot refuse her. After all, she has helped them in similar times of need.

Think for a moment about how it feels for her friends to be on the receiving end of one of those Asks? In most cases, it is true the person cannot say no. Their relationship with your board member, whether professional or personal, would make it very awkward to refuse. In their minds, their contribution is more akin to a business expense. The times I have been 'strong-armed' by my friends on boards, I have had to say yes. But as soon as my friend goes off that board, I stop giving to that organization. It is not because it was a bad organization. On the contrary, they were almost certainly doing very good work. Had they taken the time to educate and cultivate me personally, I could have become a lifelong supporter in my own right. But in their minds, I was my friend's contact, so they left me alone, not wanting to intrude.

In terms of their love of fund raising, a basic random sampling of board members will pretty much mirror a sampling of the larger population. In other words, fund raising is just not everyone's favorite activity. The same folks who may be brilliant at strategic planning or human resources may not feel they have the knack for fund raising. Remember, you didn't initially recruit all of them for their fund-raising expertise. That would be akin to asking all board members to be responsible for reviewing the annual audit in detail or securing the next real estate transaction for the organization.

On the other hand, there is a portion of the population that actually likes to ask others for money. Those are the folks you intentionally recruited to fill the fund-raising slots. You put them on the Development Committee. At the proper point in the fund raising/cultivation cycle, these folks will be of great help in asking for money, but not until potential donors have been to a Point of Entry event, received a Follow-Up Call, and been cultivated sufficiently to be ready to be asked for money.

As most of us have learned the hard way, pressuring board members to do fund raising does not work. It is a vestige of the old fund-raising reality. Even if they say they will make those three calls, many never seem to get around to it. For some, their attendance at meetings slacks off and eventually they withdraw or resign from the board feeling guilty, inadequate and frustrated.

The Three Key Roles for All Board Members in Fund Raising in the New Reality

In the new fund-raising reality, using our model, what are the roles for all board members that will enhance and support your commitment to make this the single-best volunteer experience they have ever had?

There are three recommended voluntary roles for board members in this model. Do not attempt to force anyone to do any of these. They are:

- Inviting people to Point of Entry events
- Thanking donors for gifts
- Giving money themselves

Inviting people to Point of Entry events: When you regard your board members as your most cherished advocates and ambassadors to the larger community, it is easy to see why this would be a key role. It should be safe to assume that anyone who is on your board, no matter how shy or how busy, has enough basic passion about your mission to be able to invite people to Point of Entry events. Once they have attended a Point of Entry event themselves, they will begin to trust the process. They will understand that a Point of Entry event is just a get-acquainted event and their friends will not be asked for money there. They will begin to invite others.

Be sure to prepare a list for each board meeting of all the Point of Entry guests in the past month along with the names of who invited them. This is another way for board members to get well-deserved recognition. You will be surprised by how many board members will want to see their names on that list next month.

Thanking donors for gifts: You will see a lot more of this activity in the new fund-raising reality. It can be done in an easy, non-threatening phone call or voice-mail message from a board member to every donor who has given over a certain dollar amount.

> "Hello, my name is _____. I'm on the board of
> _____. I'm calling to thank you for your generous
> gift. We really appreciate your support."

That is it. You provide the board members with names of donors and let them make the calls at any time they find convenient. If they call during the day, they can leave this thank you as a message on an answering machine or voice-mail. If, heaven forbid, they should reach the real person, odds are the person will be friendly and say nice things about the organization. If the donor called has critical feedback, you certainly want to hear it.

Have the board members report on their thank-you calls at the board meeting. This is an easy way to have them remember why they got involved with your organization in the first place. And it allows them to look good to their fellow board members without having done a tremendous amount of work. Having board members make these personal thank-you calls also will make a huge difference with the donors. Think of the message it sends: "We noticed that you gave. We appreciate it. We needed it. Please give again." It can be an essential ingredient in building lifelong donors.

Giving money themselves: By now, most nonprofit organizations have had enough basic training about boards to know it is a good idea to spell out your expectations for giving and getting (for that matter, all your expectations) to potential board members before they sign on.

Most organizations have some suggested guidelines regarding board giving. For some, it is "give, get, or get off." In other words, getting others to contribute can substitute for the board members giving themselves. Other organizations accept in-kind contributions of goods and services to substitute for a personal financial contribution. In some organizations, a corporate gift is acceptable for board members representing those corporations. Still others permit corporate contributions to underwrite a table at the annual gala to count as a board member's gift.

In this model for building a self-sustaining individual giving program, board members must give. And they must give personally through cash, stock, or some type of annual unrestricted gift, preferably in one of the multiple-year giving categories you have established. Structure it any way you like. Just make it clear you want to be able to tell other donors and the community in general, that 100% of your board gives.

After working with many organizations, I recommend that you not have an agreed-upon minimum dollar contribution. Since people's capacity to give covers a wide financial span, you run the risk of embarrassing some people into giving more than they are comfortable giving, while folks at the top end may not want to flaunt a larger gift.

Just let it be known from the beginning that the expectation at your organization is that 100% of your board gives, personally. For most board members, this will come as no surprise. And for many, once they hear they don't have to go out and solicit their friends, they will feel sufficiently relieved to be even more generous.

Here is a suggested scenario for handling board giving at a board meeting:

1. Have the Chair of your Development Committee (your designated, passionate fund raiser) on the agenda to talk about the upcoming Annual Campaign.

2. She says something like: "It's that time of year—the time when we ask all of our supporters to make their annual gift to the organization. As you recall, we each agreed when we joined the board to make a personal contribution annually. Please think about the gift you'd like to make. Over the next week or two, I will be giving each of you a call to discuss your gift."

3. At that same board meeting, she might want to give them a copy of your standard pledge card, specifying the Multiple-Year Units of Service you have adopted. It will be a good take-home reminder of the call they will soon receive.

Remember to treat your board members as you would treat every other significant major donor. Give them the one-on-one, personal attention that enhances their involvement. Show them the utmost respect and care. Then they will want to become your most stalwart lifelong donors. In addition to giving, they will introduce their friends and colleagues who, in turn, will become loyal lifelong donors. Your board members are a gift to your organization.

Consider Starting an Honorary Advisory Committee

If you are looking for a quick way to leap frog your fund-raising program into the new reality without ruffling too many feathers, you might consider starting an Honorary Advisory Committee.

This is a particularly good solution for people who are tired of waiting for the board of directors to get excited about fund raising. Do you feel as if you are constantly badgering board members to call you back, only to hear their excuses for not having followed through? Are you frustrated with not having direct access to the folks you need so you can talk up your good work?

Relax, take a deep breath, and do yourself a favor: *Give up on them.* That's right, give up. Accept the worst case scenario: They will never change. They will never be the "dream" board you had hoped for. They will never fully jump into the fund-raising area. Let it go.

Don't even criticize them for it. They are good people. They joined your board for the right reasons. Maybe fund raising was just never their thing. Maybe they have lost interest or gotten busy with other commitments. Let them off the hook and get on with it.

If you are the staff person in charge of fund raising, it is *your* job. You are the one being paid to make it happen, not the board. Unless you are anticipating a very short tenure in your job, you had better get creative.

I recommend setting up an Honorary Advisory Committee—the parallel universe structure for nonprofit organizations serious about increasing their fund-raising results exponentially.

An Honorary Advisory Committee is a breath of fresh air for everyone. There are no big time commitments, no formal money commitments, no meetings. These committee "members" agree to let you talk to them three or four times a year for advice. They are your own high-level kitchen cabinet, people who adore the organization but do not have the time or personal need to be officially involved.

You have to realize in this new reality everyone is busy. Even if they say they will help you, for the most part, that does not mean they want to run the show. They want to give you advice and let you do the legwork. They want to feel as though their contribution of time is just one piece of the larger equation. They definitely want to make a difference, but they like to keep their involvement loose. Under those circumstances, on their terms, they will be delighted to help you.

Here is how it works:

Start by making a list of the people in the community who seem to really like your program. Ideally, they have expressed this by giving you money, time, or both. Then add some of the potential major donors you have not gotten around to contacting yet, and others from your Treasure Map who would naturally have a reason to want to get involved.

Now go back through the list and put a star next to the names of people you would love to work with. You know you could learn so much from them. You would respect their advice. Their perspective and experience would add a whole new dimension to your program. You would be honored to get to know them.

Remember, in the new reality, you have given up any interest in suffering. It is fine for you to enjoy this project, to enjoy learning from the fascinating people you are working with and from the challenges you are able to tackle thanks to their collective input. Since this Honorary Advisory Committee is your own creation, pick the people you would love to work with. It is your fantasy board come true.

Did you ever take a class in college that was graded either "pass" or "fail"? In other words, you were not trying to get a good grade. You just took it to learn and enjoy. The irony is that in most pass-fail classes, the students study more and work harder than they would for a class where they receive a letter grade.

The same psychology prevails here. Let's say I agree to sign on to your Honorary Advisory Committee as my personal, extra-curricular, indulgence. I don't have to do anything other than talk to you once in awhile. Since I like you and your organization, and I can see you are an eager learner with a fervor for making something big happen, I start to enjoy it even more than I expected.

When you come by to get my advice, the meetings last a little longer than we had scheduled. I find myself thinking of strategies to help you accomplish your goal. I am noticing articles and books on your topic. I talk about it in casual conversation with my friends and family. Now I find myself looking forward to your next call.

At some point down the road, you mention that there are others on this "committee." You start telling me a little about their backgrounds. They are from all over the country, all over the world. They each have fascinating interests and experience and a passion for the same cause.

Just watch: At some point soon thereafter, one of these distinguished individuals will suggest "getting all of us together" for a think-tank type session to grapple with some issue or this campaign in person. You put together a mini-retreat with the full Honorary Advisory Committee. It is strictly an optional event at a unique, rather elegant location. There is plenty of quality down-time for folks to mingle. A few key questions are posed at the beginning. These should be the loftier questions: How to grow the Endowment Fund to the next level? How to pull in new supporters of their caliber? How to get the political support needed for your issue?

Your inspirational founder or director arrives for part of the weekend to share his or her vision and to listen. This is the advisory committee's retreat. It is not too heavily staffed. Let the group generate some recommendations. No doubt, being action-oriented, they will suggest some goals and timelines and offer to contact some folks. In the meantime, their checks will start to arrive. They know what you need and, since you are truly listening to their input, they want to help. Give this a year or two and you will have developed a cadre of senior advisors envied by all.

Don't be surprised if one or two of them start to ask about your board. At a certain point, some of them may choose to join the board, simultaneously. They'll feel more comfortable coming on the board with people of their own caliber whom they already know. Plus, if you bring on a few of them at once, it will alter the quality of your board markedly—giving you less and less to complain about!

CHAPTER 26

ADJUSTING YOUR VISION TO THE NEW REALITY: WHERE TO BEGIN

By now, I hope you can see that this model could work for you. It makes sense. It should highlight for you the many things your organization has been doing right, as well as bring to light those areas that could be tweaked a little, changed substantially, or done away with altogether.

This book is intended to transform the way you see raising funds. If we were to liken it to getting a new pair of prescription eyeglasses, we would know to expect that it might take a few days before our eyes could focus comfortably. It may take some time before we stop reaching for the old prescription pair in certain circumstances. It may take months or years before we would ever throw the old glasses away permanently.

If the Raising More Money message has sunk in, the mental template of old reality/new reality will have become familiar. Eventually it will become second nature. Asking strangers for money, "cold," will forever set off alarm bells and red flags. Putting on events that do nothing to showcase your work will become a thing of the past. Every event, meeting, or one-on-

one conversation will become an opportunity for a Point of Entry or Re-Entry. You will know that your job is to connect friends and donors to the passion and emotion of your work in addition to giving them the facts. You will recognize that you have no right to expect a true contribution from someone who has not been informed, inspired, listened to, and involved. You will know to let the donor determine the timing and pace of the relationship, ever vigilant of the donor's readiness to give again. You will know that the natural tendency of every person who has made a true contribution is to want to share that experience with others.

While eventually you will become comfortable with your new way of seeing the world, initially the challenge may seem daunting. *You don't have to overhaul everything at once.* Especially if you anticipate opposition, start by setting your sights on one area, program, or event you now offer and see how you could bring this approach, this way of seeing, to it.

Perhaps it is your annual recognition dinner, the golf tournament, or just those dreary board meetings you would like to tweak. Wearing your new glasses, you will know just what to do. When you think about that direct-mail appeal you have going out next month, you will see ways to focus on a subset of the recipients with whom you could try this approach.

Some groups start by focusing on one aspect of the model. If you are particularly in need of developing new donors, you might want to focus on Points of Entry. Set up a schedule for having at least one official Point of Entry each month. Then identify every other occasion where someone in your organization interfaces with someone in the outside public. How could those opportunities be turned into natural Points of Entry? How can you insure that the content and impact of the message are consistent? Turn it into a system.

Others find they have no shortage of friends and donors. Their issue is getting to know them better as individuals. For those organizations the focus needs to be on follow up. What if you became obsessed with doing impeccable follow up after every contact with a donor or potential donor? What if each follow-up conversation was an opportunity to elicit their personal feedback with an eye to offering them more of precisely what interests them? After six months to a year, that single focus would translate directly to your bottom line. After five years, you would have grown your base of long-term supporters exponentially.

Or perhaps you will choose to focus on asking. You may realize you have done more than enough in-depth cultivation and listening, yet no one has asked these loyal supporters to give in a big way. Then you are ready to zero in on establishing your Multiple-Year Giving Society with higher Units of Service. Put together a Challenge Gift matching fund and launch the program in a major way. You will be letting your loyal supporters know that now is the time to begin making their bigger gifts to you. You will finally be giving them the opportunity to contribute on a level commensurate with their passion about your work. Often they will wonder what has taken you so long to ask.

You may find that the only missing element of your program is giving your loyal donors a chance to introduce thers. Your pool of donors, although large and generous, has stagnated over time. Your well-established, beloved organization is ready for an infusion of new energy. Beef up your Free Feel-Good Cultivation Events, encourage those cherished supporters to invite along a new friend or two. Encourage them to bring their families to a Point of Entry. Once there, tell them about the innovative new programs you are offering. Do the careful listening in the Follow-Up Call that will tell you how best to involve them. It will make the person who introduced them to you very happy.

This new potential donor may have come to the Point of Entry or Point of Re-Entry strictly to please their friend. But by the time they choose to give, they will have been so well taken care of and so powerfully connected and reconnected to the aspect of your mission that most inspires them, that they will be delighted to give.

They will have raised their hands, and at least figuratively said, "Hey, look at me over here, you can count me in as part of the family. I want to be a part of the work you are doing. I really do understand what you're up to. Keep talking to me and teaching me more about the issues and involving me more, and I will keep giving."

You will have established, one donor at a time, a base of lifelong supporters.

You will finally be able to cast off those old eyeglasses. Your new prescription will feel perfectly normal. You will wonder what all the fuss was about. It will all seem so clear, so obvious.

What you will be seeing is the new reality.

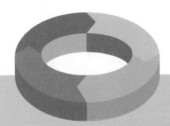

A ROAD MAP FOR GETTING STARTED

- Start by remembering back to the legacy question we asked in the beginning: "If you knew this was going to be your last year with your organization, what would you want to make happen before you could turn over your job and walk away?" How did you answer that question? What is the legacy you would want to leave?

- Then, compose your organization's team for implementing this model. Only invite people who want to be a part of this. It will most likely be a mixed group of board, staff and volunteers.

  One-on-one with you, or together in the larger group at your first meeting, have every person answer that same legacy question for themselves. What is their self-interest in leaving a self-sustaining individual giving program as a legacy? What would that provide for the organization in the way of programs, staffing, and mission fulfillment? What is the legacy they would most want to leave?

  Be sure they are very focused on why it would be worth it to them to do the work it will take to build this system. Do not go forward until each team member has a clear focus on that result. It is fine if the result is different for each person.

- Next, have a meeting of your team. Walk them through the circle model for building your lifelong donors. Be sure they understand that in the new fund-raising reality we will not ask for money until the donors are well informed and involved. Use the ripened fruit analogy.

- Suggest that you start by designing your Point of Entry event and trying it out with a few insiders and guests. Work on the best way to convey the Facts, the Emotion, and Capture the Names. Get it down to under an hour. Have a few of these events to test out different locations and program formats.

- Do the Treasure Map exercise with your team. Take half a day in a retreat-like setting to flesh out all the aspects of your Treasure Map. If you do this as a group, it will be very rich and diverse. Everyone will be part of its creation. It will become obvious to all that your organization has an abundance of treasure right under its nose. Now you just need to convert those folks to Point of Entry guests and get them going round the circle with you.

- Set up your system for the entire model. Identify all four parts:

  1. How is your Point of Entry system going to work? Who will be in charge of it? How will you get the machinery going so that new guests show up every week or month?

  2. Who will do the Follow-Up Calls? Where will all that good data be stored? Who will insure that we have taken all the necessary action steps to follow through on the suggestions from each potential donor? Who will be their ongoing Donor Services Representative?

  3. Where will the Ask take place? Who will do the asking? What will be your Units of Service or gift levels? For how many years must donors pledge to become a part of your Multiple-Year Society?

  4. How can your happy, multiple-year donors introduce others? What occasions will you offer for Free Feel-Good Cultivation Events? Can new donors host other Points of Entry events?

In other words, how will the whole system hang together so that when you come back to visit 20 years from now, you will see a well-funded organization with happy donors? The legacies that you and your team members had wanted to leave will be there, generating lifelong donors who are as committed to fulfilling on the mission of the organization as you were, way back when.

BIBLIOGRAPHY

Barker, Joel. *Paradigms: The Business of Discovering the Future.* Harper Business, 1993.

Beckwith, Harry. *Selling the Invisible: A Field Guide to Modern Marketing.* Warner Books, 1997.

Bell, Chip R. and Zemke, Ron. *Managing Knock Your Socks Off Service.* AMACOM, American Management Association, 1992.

Bowles, Sheldon. *Raving Fans.* Morrow, 1993.

Brehony, Kathleen A. *Ordinary Grace.* Riverhead Books, 1999.

Burnett, Ken. *Relationship Fundraising: A Donor-Based Approach To The Business of Raising Money.* The White Lion Press Limited London, 1992.

Cameron, Julia. *The Artist's Way: A Spiritual Path to Higher Creativity.* Jeremy P Tarcher/Putnam, 1992.

Cialdini, Robert B., Ph.D. *Influence: The Psychology of Persuasion.* Quill William Morrow, 1984.

Davis, Stan and Meyer, Christopher. *Blur: The Speed of Change in the Connected Economy,* Addison Wesley, 1998.

Eyre, Linda and Richard. *Teaching Your Children Values.* Fireside, 1993.

Glanz, Barbara A. *Building Customer Loyalty*. McGraw-Hill, 1994.

Godin, Seth. *Permission Marketing*. Simon & Schuster, 1999.

Gurin, Maurice. *Advancing Beyond the Techniques in Fund Raising*. Fund Raising Institute. Division of the Taft Group, 1991.

Hyde, Lewis. *The Gift: Imagination and the Erotic Life of Property*. Vintage Books, 1979.

Independent Sector. *Giving and Volunteering in the United States*. 1999.

Jensen, Rolf. *The Dream Society: How the Coming Shift from Information to Imagination Will Transform Your Business*. McGraw Hill, 1999.

Kaplan, Ann E., Editor. *Giving USA: The Annual Report on Philanthropy for the Year 1995*. American Association of Fund-Raising Counsel (AAFRC) Trust for Philanthropy, 1996.

Klein, Kim. *Fundraising for Social Change* (3rd edition). Chardon Press, 1994.

Lansdowne, David. *Fund Raising Realities Every Board Member Must Face*. Emerson and Church, 1996.

LeBoeuf, Michael, Ph.D. *How To Win Customers and Keep Them For Life*. New York. Berkeley Books, 1987.

Levinson, Jay Conrad. *Guerrilla Marketing Excellence: The Fifty Golden Rules For Small-Business Success*. Houghton Mifflin Company, 1993.

Levitt, Theodore. *The Marketing Imagination*. The Free Press, 1983.

McKenna, Regis. *Relationship Marketing: Successful Strategies for the Age of the Customer*. Perseus Books, 1991.

Morison, Bradley G, and Dalgleish, Julie Gordon. *Waiting in the Wings: A Larger Audience for the Arts and How to Develop It*. American Council for the Arts, 1987.

Nichols, Judith E., Ph.D., CFRE. *By the Numbers: Using Demographics and Psychographics for Business Growth in the '90s*. Bonus Books, 1990.

_____ *Changing Demographics: Fund Raising in the 1990s*. Bonus Books, 1990.

_____ *Global Demographics: Fund Raising for a New World*. Bonus Books, 1995.

_____ *Growing from Good to Great: Positioning your fund-raising efforts for BIG gains*. Bonus Books, 1995.

_____ *Pinpointing Affluence: Increasing Your Share of Major Donor Dollars*. Precept Press, 1994.

_____ *Targeted Fund Raising: Defining and Refining Your Development Strategy*, Bonus Books, 1991

O'Connell, Brian. *America's Voluntary Spirit*. The Foundation Center, 1983.

_____ *Philanthropy in Action*. The Foundation Center, 1987.

Ostrower, Francie. *Why the Wealthy Give: The Culture of Elite Philanthropy*. Princeton University Press, 1995.

Panas, Jerold. *Mega Gifts: Who gives them, who gets them*. Pluribus Press Inc, 1984.

Peppers, Don and Rogers, Martha, Ph.D. *The One to One Future: Building Relationships One Customer at a Time*. A Currency Paperback, Doubleday, 1993.

Peters, Tom. *Thriving on Chaos*. Harper Perennial, 1987.

Rabinowitz, Alan. *Social Change Philanthropy in America*. Quorum Books, 1990.

Ramsey, Karen, *Everything You Know About Money is Wrong: Overcoming the Financial Myths Keeping You from The Life You Want*. Regan Books, 1999.

Rosenberg, Claude, Jr. *Wealthy and Wise—How You and America Can Get the Most Out of Your Giving*. Little, Brown and Company, 1994.

Shaw, Sondra C. and Taylor, Martha A. *Reinventing Fundraising: Realizing the Potential of Women's Philanthropy*. Jossey-Bass, 1995.

Sharpe, Robert F., Sr. *Planned Giving Simplified*. NSFRE/Wiley Fund Development Series, 1999.

Sherden, William S. *Market Ownership: The Art & Science of Becoming #1*. AMACOM, American Management Association, 1994.

Shore, Bill. *The Cathedral Within*. Random House, 1999.

Stanley, Thomas J., Ph.D. *Marketing to the Affluent*. McGraw-Hill, 1988.

_____ *Networking with the Affluent*. McGraw-Hill, 1993.

_____ *Selling to the Affluent*. McGraw-Hill, 1991.

Steckel, Richard, Ph.D. and Lehman, Jennifer. *In Search of America's Best Nonprofits*. Jossey-Bass, 1997.

Vavra, Terry G., Ph.D. *AfterMarketing: How to Keep Customers for Life through Relationship Marketing*. McGraw-Hill, 1992.

von Schlegell, Abbie J. and Fisher, Joan M., Editors. *Women as Donors, Women as Philanthropists*. New Directions for Philanthropic Fundraising, Jossey-Bass, Inc., No. 2, Winter 1993.

Terry Axelrod, the creator of the Raising More Money workshops, trains and coaches nonprofit organizations, nationally and internationally, in how to build self-sustaining individual giving programs.

As an accomplished fund raiser, founder of three charitable organizations, and professional social worker, Terry is committed to abundant funding for the vital work of the nonprofit sector. She has been raising funds for organizations for the past 25 years. Like many fund development professionals, she began with no formal training or experience, out of the need to raise funds for a home health care program which she co-founded in the mid-1970's. Beginning with a seemingly unrelated special event, the running of the modern-day Greek Marathon, she learned by trial and error what it takes to convert one-time, "special event" donors into true, lifelong donors.

Subsequently she served as the first Director of Development at the Graduate School of Social Work at the University of Washington. Then, for 12 years, she worked in the private sector as a securities broker-dealer for a national investment firm and continued fund raising for several organizations as a volunteer.

From 1992 to 1995 she worked with Zion Preparatory Academy, an exceptional inner-city school in Seattle, Washington, that had never before done any formal fund raising. Focusing intently on individual giving, the school raised more than $7 million for unrestricted operating support and a capital campaign and was nationally recognized in a *Chronicle of Philanthropy* cover story.

Realizing that this small, relatively unknown school had been a beneficiary of individual funding of unprecedented magnitude, Terry set about to distinguish the principles that had made all that fund raising seem relatively effortless. The result is the Raising More Money model, which is now taught in an intensive three-day workshop with subsequent coaching sessions to insure its successful implementation in organizations of all types and sizes.

For more information about the Raising More Money programs or to contact Terry Axelrod directly:

Visit Terry's extensive Web site, www.raisingmoremoney.com, which offers many additional resources on this approach to individual giving. You may subscribe to her free bi-weekly electronic newsletter, the Raising More Money E-New$, by visiting the site.

Please consider submitting questions by clicking on the "Ask Terry" section of the Web site. Anecdotes and examples of what has been working as you implement this model are always welcomed.

The Web site also includes information about how to sign-up for the Raising More Money Basic and Advanced Workshops as well as order a variety of books, articles, tapes and CDs on this subject.

INDEX

RAISING MORE MONEY®

A Step-by-Step Guide to Building Lifelong Donors

CHECK YOUR LEADING BOOKSTORE OR ORDER HERE

Quantity

	BOOK: **Raising More Money®:** *A Step-by-Step Guide to Building Lifelong Donors* at $36.95 each	
	VIDEO: **An Introduction to Raising More Money®** (77 minutes) at $69.95 each	
	U.S. Shipping: $4.00 for the first item and $2.00 for each additional item	
	Sales Tax: WA residents only add $3.18 per book and $6.02 per video	
	Total	

My check or money order for $_____ is enclosed.

Please charge my: ❑ Visa   ❑ MasterCard

Orders outside the United States must be paid for by credit card.
Additional shipping costs will be added.

Name _____

Organization _____

Address _____

City/State/Zip _____

Phone_____ Email _____

Card # _____

Exp. Date_____ Signature _____

Please make your check payable and return to:
Boylston Books Ltd.
1315 Madison, #434 • Seattle, WA 98104
Call your credit card order to: 888-322-9357
Fax: 206-324-8555